CW01019836

LITERATURE

LI CHUNYU

 China Intercontinental Press

图书在版编目（ＣＩＰ）数据

中国文化·文学：英文 / 李春雨著；译谷译 . -- 北京：五洲传播出版社，2014.1
ISBN 978-7-5085-2736-9

Ⅰ.①中… Ⅱ.①李…②译… Ⅲ.①文化史—中国—英文②中国文学—文学史—英文 Ⅳ.① K203 ② I209

中国版本图书馆 CIP 数据核字 (2014) 第 067643 号

- -

中国文化系列丛书

主　　　编：王岳川
出　版　人：荆孝敏
统　　　筹：付　平

中国文化·文学

著　　　者：李春雨
译　　　者：译　谷
责 任 编 辑：苏　谦
图 片 提 供：CFP　FOTOE　东方 IC
装 帧 设 计：丰饶文化传播有限责任公司
出 版 发 行：五洲传播出版社
地　　　址：北京市海淀区北三环中路 31 号生产力大楼 B 座 7 层
邮　　　编：100088
电　　　话：010-82005927，82007837
网　　　址：www.cicc.org.cn
承 印 者：北京利丰雅高长城印刷有限公司
版　　　次：2014 年 1 月第 1 版第 1 次印刷
开　　　本：889×1194mm 1/16
印　　　张：14.75
字　　　数：200 千字
定　　　价：128.00 元

Contents

PART TWO
CHINESE MODERN AND
CONTEMPORARY LITERATURE

Preface:
Chinese Literature Going Global – The Significance of the Prize Won by Mo Yan to the History of Literature

On October 11, 2012, the Swedish Academy awarded that year's Nobel Prize in Literature to Chinese writer Mo Yan. For the development of Chinese literature, this event cannot be underestimated. Mo Yan became the first Chinese writer to win the Nobel Prize in Literature, and ended China's history of winning no Nobel Prize in Literature. This shows that Chinese literature is going global and gradually winning attention and recognition of world literature from a special angle. The prize won this time not only made a dream of Chinese literary circles come true, but also made Chinese people treat the "Nobel Prize" calmly. Meanwhile, Chinese literature also strengthened reflection on its development. According to

At the 2012 Nobel Prize Award Ceremony, Chinese writer Mo Yan received the Nobel Prize in Literature from the King of Sweden.

Nobel Committee's prize announcement, Mo Yan in his novels "with hallucinatory realism merges folk tales, history and the contemporary," and his reflection on history and analysis of human nature moved not only Chinese people, but also readers in other countries. This shows that the literature that can transcend time and national boundaries is the literature focusing on real life and writing about people's souls instead of the literature expressing political views or catering to the book market and consumption culture. Apart from Mo Yan, many contemporary Chinese writers with unique personalities have creative strength and potential such as Jia Pingwa, Chen Zhongshi, Wang Anyi, Yu Hua, Su Tong, Liu Zhenyun, Bi Feiyu and Chi Zijian. Their works contain different perceptions of life, and build their spiritual homes from different perspectives. There are also a lot of overseas readers of their works.

In view of the remoter history, Chinese literature can at least be traced to more than 3,000 years ago. From that time to the early 20th century, Chinese ancient literature came down in one continuous line, lasted thousands of years, nourished the souls of Chinese people of all generations, and established the Chinese nation's cultural identity. In the early 20th century, all-round transformation of Chinese literature took place, including literary concepts, contents and language and even the relationship with world literature. Thus Chinese literature entered a new stage.

In the new century, with the continuous enhancement of China's overall strength and gradual improvement of China's international status, more and more people began to pay attention to China. The deepening of China's reform and opening up also promoted exchange between China and the world, laying a good foundation for Chinese literature to further go global. As an important component of Chinese culture, Chinese literature enters the arena of world literature and merges with world culture continuously. Literature carries China's profound history, reflects the complex and changeful reality of today's Chinese society, and embodies Chinese people's dream of a better future. Literature is the best spiritual garden for communication between China and the world. Manifesting the whole world's common concerns and displaying the whole mankind's human feelings and human nature should be Chinese literature's responsibilities.

Since ancient times, this has been a tradition of Chinese literature.

Overview of the Development of Chinese Ancient Literature

Literature occupied an important and unique position in ancient China. Cao Pi, Emperor Wen of Wei (on the throne from 220 to 226), said "writing is a great cause of administering a country and a great event of eternity," thinking literature was an important matter bearing on the governance of the country and posterity. Ancient China's imperial examination system was also very important in selecting officials according to literary standards, especially the poem and article writing ability. China's literary traditions with a long history shaped unique literary concepts and artistic methods in their development, and exerted far-reaching influence on the literature of later ages. Ancient Chinese literary genres such as poems, essays, novels and dramas gradually improved and matured in different historical stages, and added numerous monumental classics to the world's literary treasure house.

Historical Course of Chinese Ancient Literature

Chinese literature has a long history. People usually take the "literary revolution" that began in 1917 as the dividing point, and call Chinese literature before 1917 Chinese ancient literature collectively. Chinese ancient literature's development course of thousands of years can be roughly divided into three historical periods: the remote ancient times (before the 3rd century AD), the middle ancient times (from the 3rd century AD to the 16th century) and the near ancient times (from the 16th century AD to the early 20th century).

Literature of the Remote Ancient Times

The first stage of the remote ancient times is pre-Qin literature, including the historical periods of the Shang Dynasty (1600 BC–1046 BC), the Western Zhou Dynasty (1046 BC–771 BC), the Spring and Autumn Period (770 BC–476 BC) and the Warring States Period (475 BC–221 BC).

One prominent characteristic of pre-Qin literature is that literature was still within the matrix of culture and was not separated from history and philosophy. Therefore, the greatest achievements of pre-Qin literature in prose include not only historical works such as *The Book of Documents*, *Chronicle of Zuo*, *Conversations of the States* and *Strategies of the Warring States*, but also philosophical writings of the Confucian School, the Taoist School, the Mohist School and other schools of thoughts such as *The Book of Changes*, *Laozi*, *Analects of Confucius*, *Mencius* and *Zhuangzi*. Another prominent achievement of pre-Qin literature is that in the field of poetry, *The Book of Songs* and *Verses of Chu* that remained glorious for generations emerged. *The Book of Songs* is China's first collection of poems, including works of the 500-plus year period from the early Zhou Dynasty to the mid Spring and Autumn Period. *Verses of Chu* is another collection of poems that emerged later. The literary forms, dialect and sounds of the Chu State (today's Hubei and Hunan) are used to describe local mountains, rivers, people, history and customs and express enthusiasm and romance. The main writer of *Verses of Chu* is Qu Yuan, the first great poet in the history of Chinese literature.

The second stage of the Remote Ancient Times is Qin and Han literature, including the historical periods of the Qin Dynasty (221 BC–206 BC), the Western Han Dynasty (206 BC–25 AD) and the Eastern Han Dynasty (25–220). Against the backdrop of political and cultural unification, Qin and Han literature lost the vigor of pre-Qin literature and showed a stereotyped and stagnant style. This is fully reflected in the most representative literary form of this period – the Han rhapsody. Most contents of Han rhapsodies exaggeratedly depict palaces, cities, emperors' hunting trips, etc. with flowery language full of detailed descriptions and parallel structures. The real representative of the highest level of Qin and Han prose is Sima Qian's biographical general history *Records of the Grand Historian*, which made outstanding achievements in the art of narration and characterization. However, poetry had new vitality. Yuefu folk songs of the Han Dynasty spreading among people and *Nineteen Ancient Poems* created by scholars of the middle and lower classes both describe parting, frustration and worries about uncertainties in life with plain language and sincerity, and can still strike a responsive chord with readers thousands of years later.

Literature of the Middle Ancient Times

Literature of the middle ancient times is literature of the historical period from the Wei Dynasty (220–265) and the Jin Dynasty (265–420) through the Southern and Northern Dynasties (420–589), the Sui Dynasty (581–618), the Tang Dynasty (618–907), the Five Dynasties (907–960), the Song Dynasty (960–1279) and the Yuan Dynasty (1271–1368) to the mid Ming Dynasty (1368–1644).

The first stage of the middle ancient times is from the Wei and Jin dynasties to the mid Tang Dynasty. Chinese literature entered the stage of consciousness from the stage of spontaneity, and in particular poem creation reached a peak. In several centuries, brilliant poets came forth in

large numbers from the "Three Caos," "Seven Scholars of Jian'an" and "Zhengshi poets" to Tao Yuanming, Xie Lingyun, Yu Xin, the "Four Great Poets of the Early Tang Dynasty," Chen Ziang, Wang Wei, Meng Haoran, Gao Shi, Cen Shen, Li Bai, Du Fu… Poets' unique personalities echo with their works' unique styles. The fervent and solemn "Jian'an style," the "voice of Zhengshi poets" infused with sorrow and joy of life and rational thinking and the magnificent and vigorous style of the "prosperous Tang Dynasty" all exerted far-reaching influence on later generations' poetry paradigms.

The second stage of the middle ancient times is from the mid Tang Dynasty to the fall of the Southern Song Dynasty. In this period, the most important event in the literary circles was the "Classical Prose Movement" advocating reform of literary styles, literary genres and literary language. This reform initiated by Han Yu in the Tang Dynasty and carried forward by Ouyang Xiu, etc. in the Song Dynasty exerted far-reaching influence on the development of Chinese prose. After reaching a climax in the prosperous Tang Dynasty and being expanded by poets of the mid and late Tang Dynasty such as Bai Juyi, Li He, Li Shangyin and Du Mu, poetry underwent new development in a different direction. Ci poetry, a new literary form shaped on the basis of poetry, attracted a lot of attention. Su Shi and Xin Qiji representing the bold and unconstrained school of ci poetry and Liu Yong and Li Qingzhao representing the graceful and restrained school of ci poetry elevated this new literary form's status to the representative of literature of the Song Dynasty together. What deserves special attention is that legends thrived after the mid and late Tang Dynasty, marking Chinese novels had entered the stage of maturity; with the prosperity of the commodity economy and the rise of the civil culture in the Song Dynasty, vernacular novels created with colloquial language emerged, completely changed the Chinese ancient literary tradition of using classical Chinese, and laid an important foundation for the development of novels in later ages in terms of language, narrative models, etc.

The third stage of the middle ancient times is from the Yuan Dynasty to the mid Ming Dynasty. In this period, narrative literature represented by novels and traditional Chinese opera began to replace poems and essays and dominate the literary circles. Yuan drama was not only a milestone in China's drama history, but also became another classic in the history of Chinese ancient literature comparable to poetry of the Tang Dynasty and ci poetry of the Song Dynasty. The emergence of the two long vernacular novels of *Romance of the Three Kingdoms* and *Water Margin* was another important symbol of this period, heralding a new epoch of literature.

Literature of the Near Ancient Times

Literature of the approximately 400-year period from the mid Ming Dynasty to the beginning of "literary revolution" in 1917 belongs to literature of the near ancient times.

The first stage of literature of the near ancient times is from the mid Ming Dynasty to the Opium War of 1840. In this period, the most prominent literary genres were no longer traditional poems and essays but popular literature represented by dramas and novels. In particular, novels continued to mature in terms of literary forms, ideological connotations, etc., and classic works such as *Journey to the West*, *Dream of the Red Chamber*, *Strange Stories from a Chinese Studio* and *The Scholars* emerged.

After the Opium War, China was gradually reduced from a feudal society to a semi-colonial and semi-feudal society. Social changes brought about changes in literary concepts and literary creation. Literature began to be deemed as a tool for improving the society, and was gradually influenced by Western literature. New thoughts and new styles germinated under the traditional framework.

The "literary revolution" that began in 1917 was part of the "May 4th" New Culture Movement. It opposed classical Chinese, advocated vernacular Chinese, opposed old literature, advocated taking new literature as a flag, and became a distinctive milestone in the history of Chinese literature. Chinese ancient literature which has lasted thousands of years ended, and Chinese literature entered a brand new era.

Main Characteristics of Chinese Ancient Literature

Unique Literary Concepts

Attaching importance to literature's sociality, practicality and display of individuals' personalities is an important basic concept of Chinese ancient literature. The Confucian classic *Analects of Confucius* emphasizes, "Poetry would ripen you; teach you insight, friendliness and forbearance." The general idea is that poetry can be used to inspire emotions, observe the society and nature, make friends and tactfully criticize or satirize injustice. It manifests a deep understanding of poetry's aesthetic functions and social and educational functions. Wang Chong (27–97), a scholar of the Han Dynasty, thought, "Essays useful to people are harmless, and those not useful to people are superfluous." Bai Yuji, a poet of the Tang Dynasty, said, "Essays are written for the sake of the times, and poems are written for the sake of events." Su Shi, a writer of the Song Dynasty, also pointed out that literature should be "created for something" and "target current malpractices." These arguments all emphasize literature's social property of "practical use." Meanwhile, there are many Chinese ancient literary works describing personal life and emotions. Take the Gong'an School and Jingling School of the Ming Dynasty for example, they clearly proposed that poems and essays should "display individuals' personalities in diverse forms." Actually, in literary practice, such works attaching importance to display of individuals' emotions and interests existed extensively in various periods, and spread more widely to a large extent.

Ancient China's unique literary concepts were deeply influenced by Confucian, Buddhist and Taoist doctrines. The Confucian School advocated "cultivating one's moral character, putting one's own house in order, running the country well and letting peace prevail on earth" and "lifting my ruler higher than Yao and Shun and restoring the purity of the people's ways," though hermits like Tao Yuanming still cherished the ideal of "greatly benefiting people in the world." The Taoist School advocated "Tao models itself after nature," freedom and naturalness. The metaphysics of the Wei and Jin dynasties was a developing form of Taoism. Buddhism as a religion, especially the Zen Sect, played an important role in adjusting frustrated ancient scholars' thoughts and mentalities.

Abundant Artistic Methods

The artistic methods of ancient Chinese literature are very abundant, and multiple methods such as blending of feelings and settings, expression of emotions through describing concrete objects, contrast, imagination, symbolization, use of idioms and puns are often used to depict characters, describe environments and express emotions. Chinese ancient literature focuses on "manifestation" instead of "reproduction" of people and things, i.e. the author reached the state of integration of things and himself according to his subjective will by selecting, abstracting and recombining in his mind external people or things.

In terms of literary criticism, Chinese ancient literature developed unique concepts such as air, rhythm, flavor, meaning, spirit, genre, style, texture, pattern and artistic conception, and formed a literary writing and evaluation system different from that of the West. In short, the highest state pursued by Chinese ancient literature is "perception by intuition instead of explanation in words" and "vivid description without one word." Though these expressions sound very mysterious and abstruse, they could be understood and evaluated by ancient Chinese writers very easily.

Separation of "Language" and "Literature"

As the main carrier of writings of Chinese ancient literature, classical Chinese was mainly used for reading and writing and was separated from everyday words and expressions in life over time. Compared with everyday language, classical Chinese is concise, elegant, simple and lively, contributed to Chinese ancient literature's stylistic feature of "conciseness," and played a key role

in the formation and development of ancient literature's sense of beauty, skills and realm. In the history of thousands of years, everyday words and expressions changed dramatically, but phrases, sentence patterns and stylistic rules of classical Chinese remained relatively stable, thus ensuring the continuity of China's literary traditions.

Though classical Chinese was Chinese ancient literature's main mode of writing, the factor of vernacular Chinese also emerged. Civil popular literature including novels and dramas mostly adopted language mixing classical Chinese and vernacular Chinese. This state lasted till the late Qing Dynasty. In the literary reform movement in the late Qing Dynasty, language reform was the main focus of the ideological and literary circles then, and the opinion that "I write what I say" gradually received extensive recognition. After the "May 4th" New Culture Movement in the early 20th century, vernacular Chinese became the main written language of Chinese literature, and combination of "language" and "literature" was realized for the first time.

Superiority of "Poems" and "Essays"

In the concepts and practices of Chinese ancient literature, "poems" and "essays" were superior literary forms. Ancient people's orthodox creations were "poems" and "essays," and novels and dramas were mostly regarded as informal works. This is notably different from Western culture and literature. Under the Western context, ancient Greek tragedies are the most sublime artistic classics. The social and cultural status of ancient Chinese novels and dramas was relatively low, and the authors of many excellent novels and dramas did not leave their names in history. Around the beginning of the 20th century, China's feudal society declined gradually. Against the backdrop of domestic trouble and foreign invasion, thinkers and writers thought highly of the huge role played by novels and dramas in enlightening people and reforming thoughts – for example, Liang Qichao wrote in *On the Relationship Between Novels and the Control of the Masses*, "The reform of the novel should come before the reform of the nation's populace." Therefore, the social status of novels and dramas gradually rose, and they became two literary genres comparable to "poems" and "essays."

Next, we will introduce important writers and works of different periods of Chinese ancient literature in more detail according to different literary genres.

Picture Scroll of Chinese Poets of Past Dynasties (part), painted by contemporary Li Junqi

Model Essays

In ancient China, the "essay" was one of the most important literary styles and the most widely used and practical literary genre. Compared with poems, novels, dramas, etc., essays pursue trueness of contents to a larger extent. In terms of linguistic forms, "essays" can be classified into parallel verse, rhymed verse and prose. These three forms developed alternately in the history of literature. Parallel verse is a literary genre that emerged after the Wei and Jin dynasties, mostly adopting the four-line and six-line patterns. It is strictly antithetical, using flowery language, excessively emphasizing forms and restricting most content expressions. Rhymed verse refers to rhymed articles written according to rhyme formats, including literary genres such as eulogies, odes, admonitions, inscriptions, laments and funeral prayers. The concept of Chinese ancient prose is very extensive. Articles other than parallel verse and rhymed verse can also be called "prose." According to different modes of expression and written contents, prose can be classified into lyric prose, narrative prose, argumentative prose, landscape and travel prose, etc.

Prose of Various Pre-Qin Schools of Thought

In the Spring and Autumn Period and Warring States Period, because wars caused a lot of chaos and China was not unified, private studies thrived and various schools' writings emerged one after another. This was the first large-scale ideological debate and academic contention in China's history called "contention of a hundred schools of thought" in later generations.

The so-called a hundred schools of thought refer to the numerous book writers of that period with great influence and diverse styles. According to the summarization in *The Book of Arts of the Chronicles of Han Dynasty*, they mainly include "ten schools:" the Confucian School, the Taoist

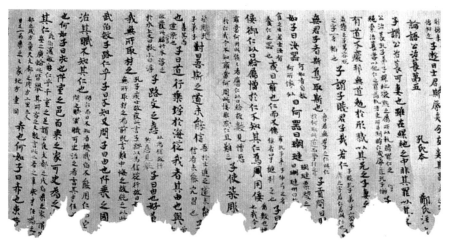

Incomplete pages of the Tang handwritten version of *Analects of Confucius* annotated by Zheng Xuan

Pictures of the Sage's Traces of the Ming Dynasty (part), depicting Confucius' life segments of retiring to compile poetry books and teaching disciples

School, the Legalist School, the Mohist School, the School of Logicians, the School of Diplomacy, the Yin-Yang School, the Agriculturist School, the School of Eclectics and the School of Minor Talks. In light of the influence in that period and later ages, the Confucian School, the Taoist School, the Legalist School and the Mohist School are more important. Various schools wrote books mainly to express views and state reasons, and most of their writings are prose. Among the academic essays of various schools, the most influential ones are *Analects of Confucius*, *Laozi*, *Zhuangzi*, etc.

Analects of Confucius

It is a book recording the words and deeds of Confucius and his disciples. Today's edition of *Analects of Confucius* consisting of 20 chapters in total began to be compiled around the early Warring States Period.

Confucius (551 BC–470 BC), with the given name of Qiu and the courtesy name of Zhongni, was a native of Zouyi in the Lu State and the founder of the Confucian School. His ancestors were aristocrats of the Song State, and later migrated to the Lu State. Confucius never achieved his ambition in his lifetime. Though he served as the Minister of Justice of the Lu State, traveled in various states and made great efforts to advocate his political opinions, he never realized his ambition. At last, he returned to the Lu State and engaged in teaching and writing. It is said that he had 3,000 disciples including 72 brilliant ones. *Analects of Confucius* systematically reflects Confucius' thoughts. The core of his thoughts is "benevolence" and "propriety." The so-called "benevolence" mainly refers to moral cultivation and ethical education; the so-called "propriety" refers to political systems, moral standards, etc. Confucius advocated "looking not at what is contrary to propriety; listening not to what is contrary to propriety; speaking not what is contrary to propriety; making no movement which is contrary to propriety," thinking that only by preserving "propriety" could the world order be maintained to "let the king be a king, the minister a minister, the father a father and the son a son."

Analects of Confucius is also of important significance with respect to education. *Analects of Confucius* vividly records Confucius' educational opinions such as teaching with tireless zeal, teaching students in accordance with their aptitude and teaching with skill and patience as well as how he practiced what he advocated. Some famous sayings such as "in education there should be no class distinctions," "knowledge is recognizing what you know and what you don't" and "learning without thought is labor lost; thought without learning is perilous" have deeply influenced Chinese people for thousands of years.

From the literary perspective, *Analects of Confucius* adopts the form of quotation-style prose with profound meanings and concise, plain, vivid, implicit and meaningful words. Even long arguments are interesting and full of strong emotion. *Analects of Confucius* also records some penetrating views of Confucius on literature and art – for example, Confucius said, "In the Book of Poetry are three hundred pieces, but the design of them all may be embraced in one sentence – 'Having no depraved thoughts.'" This view exerted far-reaching influence on the development of Chinese literature in later ages.

Laozi

Laozi, with the surname of Li, the given name of Er, the courtesy name of Dan and the alias of Laodan, lived in the Chu State in the Spring and Autumn Period, and was the founder of the Taoist School. According to later scholars' textual research, the book *Laozi* was written not by Laozi, but by his students. Today's version of *Laozi* consists of 81 chapters. The first volume is *Tao Classic* including 37 chapters, and the second volume is *Virtue Classic* including 44 chapters. Therefore, *Laozi* is also called *Tao Te Ching.*

Laozi contains only 5,000 Chinese characters, but is abstruse and profound, epitomizing Laozi's complete philosophical thought system. "Tao" and "nature" are the core of Laozi's philosophy. He emphasized, "the Tao that can be spoken is not the eternal Tao," "the name that can be named is not the eternal name" and "humans follow the laws of Earth; Earth follows the laws of Heaven; Heaven follows the laws of Tao; Tao follows the laws of nature." What Laozi called "Tao" is not human will or social systems but universal principles and fundamental laws governing the existence and change of all things in the world – the "Tao" of "nature." "Tao" proposed by Laozi marked a very high level of man's understanding of all things on earth and a new peak of China's philosophical development. Laozi's "laws of nature" not only emphasize the life philosophy of "nature and non-action" and "governing by doing nothing," but also are quite dialectic:

Picture of Laozi on a Cow, painted by Chao Buzhi in the Song Dynasty. It is said that Laozi, seeing the decline of the royal family of the Zhou Dynasty, left on a cow and disappeared.

Photo of *Tao Te Ching*

Qing (Guangxu) block-printed edition of *Zhuangzi*

Misfortune is what fortune depends upon; fortune is where misfortune hides beneath.

Nothing in the world is softer or weaker than water, yet nothing is better at overcoming the hard and strong. This is because nothing can replace it. That the weak overcomes the strong and the soft overcomes the hard. Everybody in the world knows but cannot put into practice.

True words are not beautiful; beautiful words are not true. Those who are good do not debate; those who debate are not good. Those who know are not broad of knowledge; those who are broad of knowledge do not know.

Laozi contains simple, concise, clear and though-provoking words. Its sentences are mostly dialectal sayings, proverbs, adages and epigrams, adding to its profound philosophical connotations and at the same time having poetic flavor.

Zhuangzi

There were 52 chapters according to *The Book of Arts of the Chronicles of Han Dynasty*, and 33 chapters exist today. It is the main representative work of the pre-Qin Taoist School. Zhuangzi (c. 369 BC–286 BC), with the courtesy name of Zhou, lived in the Song State in the mid Warring States Period. Zhuangzi's studies belonged to the category of the Taoist School, but he inherited and further developed the thought of Laozi. From Confucius to Laozi and Zhuangzi, we can see different tracks of China's political and philosophical development. Confucius "did something even though it was impossible," Laozi "did nothing to do everything," and Zhuangzi "did nothing" or "did not act." It seems that Zhuangzi's thought is relatively negative and void. He pursued absolute spiritual freedom and complete transcendence from real society and imagined a spiritual state not restricted by any condition. However, what is more manifested by Zhuangzi's philosophy is the pursuit of ideals. For example, he particularly emphasized "the perfect man cares for no self; the holy man cares for no merit; the sage cares for no name." This is a typical state of ideal personalities. Confucius' realistic approach had progressive significance, Laozi's abstruse approach conformed to nature and had important value, and Zhuangzi's idealistic approach had the unique effect of transcending reality.

Besides, the more important value of *Zhuangzi* lies in the artistic charm of its prose. People often describe the free and transcendent literary style of Zhuangzi's prose as "powerful and unstrained like a heavenly steed soaring across the skies," and weird artistic images are also a unique characteristic of Zhuangzi's prose. The huge fish and roc, the butterfly that Zhuangzi became in his dream, Zhi Lishu the Lame whose body was incomplete, the stonemason who whirled the hatchet with a noise like the wind, etc. were all written by Zhuangzi with inspiration. This strange style of conception and writing makes *Zhuangzi* a glorious representative of the prose of a hundred schools of thought.

Picture of the Butterfly Dream, painted by Liu Guandao in the Yuan Dynasty, is based on *Zhuangzi – The Adjustment of Controversies*: Zhuangzi dreamed that he became a butterfly and did not know after waking up whether he became a butterfly or a butterfly became Zhuangzi.

Sima Qian and Records of the Grand Historian

Sima Qian (c. 145 BC–87 BC), with the courtesy name of Zichang, lived in the Western Han Dynasty. He began to read classics in his childhood, travelled around China at the age of 20, toured with Emperor Wu many times, was ordered to serve as an envoy in the southwest, and succeeded his father as the Court Astrologer at the age of 38. Sima Qian's completion of *Records of the Grand Historian* was closely related to these spot surveys, his life experiences, his thorough understanding of ancient and current history, his familiarity with cultural classics and customs, his knowledge about astronomy, geography and ethnic customs, etc.

Figure of Sima Qian

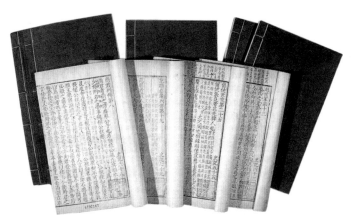

Photo of *Records of the Grand Historian*

In the 2nd year of the Tianhan Period (99 BC), Sima Qian was imprisoned for defending Li Ling's defeat and surrender to Huns, and suffered humiliating castration. After being released from prison, Sima Qian continued to write *Records of the Grand Historian* despite his mental and physical agony. Imprisonment and humiliation greatly influenced Sima Qian's life and his writing of *Records of the Grand Historian*. In this period, he wrote a famous article entitled *Letter to Ren An* to recount Emperor Wu's lack of sympathy with pain, expose jailers' cruelty, analyze people's snobbishness and unreservedly express the attitude and purpose of writing *Records of the Grand Historian*: the history of more than 3,000 years recorded by *Records of the Grand Historian* is for "investigating patterns of the nature and human society and understanding the changes of both ancient times and present." This shows that Sima Qian wrote *Records of the Grand Historian* to explore great changes in the history of 3,000 years and probe into the causes and consequences of these changes. It not only records history, but also contemplates and reflects on history.

The style of Sima Qian's book *Records of the Grand Historian*, his attitude towards treatment of history and his articles' literary form were all of important pioneering significance and exerted far-reaching influence on later generations.

First, the first biographical history *Records of the Grand Historian* systematically and comprehensively reveals historical events, describes and depicts historical figures' images and exposes the essence and connotations of historical development from the five aspects of imperial biographies, treatises, tables, biographies of the feudal houses and eminent persons, and biographies and collective biographies. Among them, imperial biographies, biographies of the feudal houses and eminent persons, and biographies and collective biographies are the main lines of *Records of the Grand Historian* focusing on people and events. Besides, "treatises" in *Records of the Grand Historian* mainly record important laws of past dynasties and their development; "tables" mainly include chronological tables of important events and chronological tables of people.

Another main aspect of the value of *Records of the Grand Historian* is Sima Qian's attitude of treating and recording history truthfully "without overstating virtues and understating evils," his critical spirit, and his clear understanding of what to love and what to hate. Sima Qian treated historical materials meticulously and cautiously, recording true materials, omitting false ones and leaving space between truth and falsehood. Thanks to this attitude and practice of refusing to fabricate history and mislead later generations, materials with true referential value were left to later people. In writing *Records of the Grand Historian*, Sima Qian never concealed his clear subjective emotions and value judgments, and manifested his intention of taking the past as a mirror of the present throughout the book. He ruthlessly denounced and criticized those deceitful, crafty, dissolute, selfish, cruel and shameless people in history, and even sharply criticized Liu Bang, the highest ruler of the Han Dynasty, and he warmly praised and eulogized those knights-errant true in word and resolute in deed, those honest people who were slandered because of their loyalty and died without regret, and those righteous people who valued justice more than life and died as martyrs. These praise and disparage embody Sima Qian's character, belief and social ideal.

Another prominent aspect of the value of *Records of the Grand Historian* is its literary achievements. It not only narrates events vividly with concise language, but also depicts people with emphasis. This represents great development in comparison with past historical books such as *Chronicle of Zuo* and *Strategies of the Warring States*. Throughout *Records of the Grand Historian*, historical materials mostly focus on people and events, and lifelike images of people reveal true history vividly. *Records of the*

The Hongmen Banquet, a critically important turning point in Xiang Yu's domination, is also the most splendid description in *The Imperial Biography of Xiang Yu*.

The end of *The Imperial Biography of Xiang Yu* describes how Xiang Yu was trapped and embattled on all sides in Gaixia, parted with his favorite concubine Yu Ji in tears, and committed suicide by cutting his own throat beside the Wu River at last. The classical Beijing opera *The King's Parting with His Favorite* is based on this.

Grand Historian not only depicts many different kinds of people, but also describes different lots and personalities of different individuals belonging to the same kind, and these people's personalities and fates make historical narratives full of ups and downs. For example, *The Imperial Biography of Xiang Yu* shows sudden changes in the period between the late Qin Dynasty and the early Han Dynasty through the heroic but tragic life of Xiang Yu. Sima Qian made efforts to shape Xiang Yu's heroic image of "having strength to lift mountains and spirit to take on the world" in the article, and meanwhile did not avoid the weaknesses in his personality such as violence, bloodthirstiness, suspicion and foolhardiness. Sima Qian, despite his in-depth criticism of these tragic people, more often felt sorry for and sympathized with them. The section "Hongmen Banquet" vividly describes many people with different shapes and personalities and fascinating dramatic conflicts arising one after another, and can be called a classic literary description.

Modern Chinese writer Lu Xun (1881–1936) called *Records of the Grand Historian* "the unique work of all historians, the songs of Qu Yuan without rhyme," highly confirming the historical and literary value of *Records of the Grand Historian*.

Eight Great Prose Masters of the Tang and Song Dynasties

Following the prose of a hundred schools of thought and *Records of the Grand Historian*, Chinese ancient prose reached another peak of development in the Tang and Song dynasties. Particularly, under the influence and push of the Classical Prose Movement in the Tang and Song dynasties, numerous writers showed their talents and brought about a new scene of prose in Tang and Song dynasties. Among them, Han Yu and Liu Zongyuan who lived in the Tang Dynasty and Ouyang Xiu, Su Xun, Su Shi, Su Zhe, Wang Anshi and Zeng Gong who lived in the Song Dynasty were quite influential for their unique styles and were historically called "Eight Great Prose Masters of the Tang and Song Dynasties". The Eight Great Prose Masters of the Tang and Song Dynasties were all important representatives of the Classical Prose Movement. They opposed parallel verse, advocated prose, emphasized the novel and natural writing style, and supported the plain and fluent literary style. Their theoretical concepts and creative practices exerted important and far-reaching influence on the development of literature, especially the change of prose, after the Tang and Song dynasties.

Han Yu

Han Yu (768–824), with the courtesy name of Tuizhi, the posthumous title of "Wen" and the alias of Han Wengong, was known as Han Changli because he was a native of Changli, Hebei. He studied hard in his childhood and served as Assistant Minister of the Department of War, Assistant Minister of the Department of Official Personnel and Governor of the Capital, but he never achieved his ambition in his lifetime despite his outstanding literary talent and political views. He wrote *Han Changli's Collected Works* consisting of 40 volumes, etc.

Han Yu's articles advocated Confucius' thoughts, and played an important role in establishing the concept of "Confucian orthodoxy" in China. In terms of literary styles, Han Yu emphasized novelty, strangeness and steady change. His articles were written with concise language, integrating classical Chinese and vernacular Chinese. For example, his articles such as *On the Teacher* are both argumentative articles and essays, which contain matter-of-fact narrations but are full of ups and downs and easy to understand with strong momentum and affinity. Du Mu (803–c. 852), a poet of the late Tang Dynasty, called Han Yu's prose and Du Fu's poetry "Du's poetry and Han's prose" collectively, showing the high status of Han Yu's prose in the history of literature.

Figure of Han Yu

Liu Zongyuan

Liu Zongyuan (773–819), with the courtesy name of Zihou, was a native of Hedong (today's Yuncheng City, Shanxi Province) and was known as Liu Hedong. He died in Liuzhou at the age of 46, so people also called him Liu Liuzhou. Liu Zongyuan wrote more than 600 poems and essays in his lifetime. His poems are outstanding, but his literary achievements and influence are greater. His main works are in *Liu Hedong's Collected Works* consisting of 45 volumes.

Liu Zongyuan and Han Yu had the same literary ambition, opposed the flowery literary style prevalent since the Six Dynasties, and actively advocated plain and fluent articles with meaningful connotations. Liu Zongyuan's prose contains lofty connotations and plain words, and his travel notes and allegories are commended for their novelty. *Eight Records of Excursions in Yongzhou* written by him after being demoted to be an official in Yongzhou is his classic work of travel prose, and *A Small Pond* in it is a widely known article. He seemed to enjoy leisure among mountains and rivers, but his mind was upset and his perceptions of life were manifested by natural scenes. His language is novel, vigorous, unsophisticated and concise. In the history of Chinese literature, *Eight Records of Excursions in Yongzhou* marked the establishment of landscape and travel prose as an independent genre. There are also some allegories in the prose created by Liu Zongyuan such as *The Rats of a Certain Family at Yongzhou*, *The Deer of Linjiang* and *The Donkey of Guizhou*, which are humorous with profound morals.

A painting created by Wu Youru in the Qing Dynasty according to Liu Zongyuan's *Biography of the Tree Planter Guo Tuotuo*. This essay explains why politicians should follow the people's wish and let the people recover on the parable of the tree planter Guo Tuotuo.

Ouyang Xiu

Ouyang Xiu (1007–1072), with the courtesy name of Yongshu, the alias of Zuiweng and the posthumous title of Wenzhong, was a politician, writer and historian of the Northern Song Dynasty often called Ouyang Wenzhong in later ages. He wrote *New History of the Tang Dynasty* with Song Qi, and compiled *History of Five Dynasties* independently. His main works are included in *Collected Works of Ouyang Wenzhong*. Ouyang Xiu made a lot of political and literary accomplishments, and actively guided the poem and essay reform movement in the Northern Song Dynasty. His political thoughts influenced the times, his poems, ci poems and essays were widely known, and Su Shi and his brothers, Zeng Gong, Wang Anshi, etc. were all his students.

Ouyang Xiu's essays express emotions and explain reasons very well, giving emphasis to both momentum and euphemism. Emotions are expressed earnestly and skilfully, and reasons are explained smoothly and fluently. *On Factions*, *History of the Five Dynasties – The Preface to Biographies of Chief Officers of Music*, *The Roadside Hut of the Old Drunkard*, *Ode to the Autumn Sound*, *Lamenting Shi Manqing*, *Old Oil Peddler*, etc. are all Ouyang Xiu's famous articles.

The Roadside Hut of the Old Drunkard in Chuzhou, Anhui. *The Roadside Hut of the Old Drunkard*, created after Ouyang Xiu was demoted to the post of Prefect of Chuzhou, depicts Chuzhou's mountain scenery and the joy felt by tourists and the author among mountains and rivers.

Tablet inscription of *The Roadside Hut of the Old Drunkard*, handwritten by Ouyang Xiu's disciple Su Dongpo

"Three Sus"

"Three Sus" is a collective term for Su Xun the father, Su Shi the elder brother and Su Zhe the younger brother. Su Xun (1009–1066), with the courtesy name of Mingyun and the alias of Laoquan, was a native of Meishan, Meizhou (today's Sichuan). His main works are included in *Jiayou Collection*. Su Xun had not only political ambitions, but also military visions. In articles such as *On Balance*, *Letter to the Emperor* and *On the Six States*, he boldly put forward his views on running the country and innovating in politics. His prose, especially political arguments, is most vigorous, trenchant and incisive, targeting current malpractices. Su Shi (1037–1101), with the courtesy name of Zizhan and the alias of Dongpo Jushi, was Su Xun's son often called Su Dongpo in later ages, and a famous writer and calligrapher of the Northern Song Dynasty. His main poems and essays are included in *Seven Collections of Dongpo*, etc. Su Shi was versatile. His poems and ci poems are unrestrained and have a style of their own, and his prose is also easy to understand and straightforward with a unique style. He and Ouyang Xiu are collectively called "Ouyang and Su." Su Zhe (1039–1112), with the courtesy name of Ziyou, was Su Shi's younger brother. Su Zhe's

The Temple of the Three Sus located in the Three Sus' hometown Meishan, Sichuan

studies and writings were deeply influenced by his father and elder brother, and his main works include *Notes on the Book of Songs*, *Spring and Autumn Annals*, *Ancient History* and *Notes on Laozi*. Su Zhe emphasized the theory of "fostering moral character," i.e. articles should be based on extensive and profound life experiences and focus on authors' inner accomplishments. His writing style is plain but magnificent, simple but rich.

Wang Anshi

Wang Anshi (1021–1086), with the courtesy name of Jiefu, was a native of Linchuan (today's Dongxiang County, Jiangxi Province) and a politician, thinker and writer of the Northern Song Dynasty. His main works are included in *Wang Linchuan Collection*, *Collected Works of Mr. Linchuan*, *Supplement of Linchuan Collection*, *Songs of Mr. Linchuan*, etc. Wang Anshi always opposed the void and weak literary style, and his literary opinion and creation were both closely related to his political ideals, emphasizing the social function of literature, which should "benefit the world." Wang Anshi created many kinds of works,

Figure of Wang Anshi

34

and excelled in poems and essays. Most of his articles are very logical and persuasive political essays expressing profound thoughts with incisive words, showing the politician's original views and broad mind. *Letter to Emperor Renzong, Letter of Reply to Sima Guang, Reading an Account of Lord Mengchang, Lament over the Oblivion of Zhongyong*, etc. are all Wang Anshi's famous works.

Zeng Gong

Zeng Gong (1019–1083), with the courtesy name of Zigu, was an active participant of the poem and essay reform movement in the Northern Song Dynasty. His work *Writings of the Yuanfeng Period* consisting of 50 volumes exists today. He made great achievements in prose creation, and formed a style of his own. Wang Anshi praised him in *To Zeng Zigu*, "Zeng Gong's articles are rare and can be compared to the Yangtze River, the Han River and the Big Dipper." Zeng Gong paid attention to "methods" instead of "genres" in writing. Essays, prefaces and letters among his articles represent his highest accomplishments. *Letter to Ouyang Xiu, Letter to the Governor of Fuzhou, Preface to the Contents of Strategies of the Warring States*, etc. have always been commended by people.

Splendid Poetry

China is a country of poems. In the long history of thousands of years, poems and essays were deemed as orthodox literature and developed along many lines. Ancient Chinese poems can be classified into archaic poems and modern poems according to meters. Archaic poems mainly refer to pre-Tang poems with unfixed numbers of sentences and Chinese characters, few metrical restrictions and free rhymes. Modern poems, which are metrical poems relative to archaic poems including metrical poems and quatrains, matured in the Tang Dynasty. A metrical poem includes eight lines, and a quatrain includes four lines. A line usually consists of five or seven Chinese characters, and there are strict rhymes. Metrical poems also require antithesis at designated positions. Ancient Chinese poems can be classified into poems on objects, poems on departure, poems on borders, poems on the past, poems on women's complaints, satirical poems, pastoral poems, etc. according to different contents; and can be classified into lyric poems and narrative poems according to different modes of content expression. In a broad sense, ancient poems include many forms such as poems, ci poems and songs.

Poems of different periods have different historical and cultural characteristics. As people usually say, the poetry of the Tang Dynasty is emotional and the ci poetry of the Song Dynasty is rational. Different regions' poems also have distinctive local features. For example, though both *The Book of Songs* and *Verses of Chu* are pre-Qin classics. The former depicts the northern region with the Yellow River basin as the center in a plain style, and the latter mainly depicts life in the Chu State in the middle and lower reaches of the Yangtze River with passionate emotion and abundant imagination.

The Book of Songs:
The First Collection of Poems

The Book of Songs is China's earliest collection of poems and the beginning of China's poetry traditions. *The Book of Songs* was called *Poetry* or *300 Poems* in the pre-Qin period. In the Han Dynasty, *Poetry* was listed as a Confucian classic and thus was called *Classic of Poetry*. Most works in *The Book of Songs* were created from the early Western Zhou Dynasty to the mid Spring and Autumn Period.

The Book of Songs consists of 311 poems, and only 305 exist. All of them can be sung with music. According different types of music, poems in *The Book of Songs* are classified into "airs," "court hymns" and "eulogies." "Airs" are mainly folk songs created by laborers; "court hymns" including "lesser court hymns" and "major court hymns" are mainly songs for imperial court meetings and banquets created by aristocratic scholars mostly; "eulogies" are mainly songs for sacrificial ceremonies in ancestral temples also created by aristocratic scholars mostly.

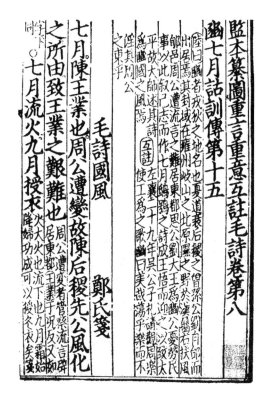

Photo of the Song block-printed edition of *The Book of Songs*, collected by the National Library of China

The *Book of Songs* contains very abundant ideological contents, involving various aspects of the life of the aristocratic class and ordinary people in the society of that period. Themes include history, praise, sarcasm, love, marriage, agriculture, enlistment, etc. *Crying Ospreys* is a famous poem:

Merrily the ospreys cry,
On the islet in the stream.
Gentle and graceful is the girl,
A fit wife for the gentleman.
Short and long the floating water plants,
Left and right you may pluck them.
Gentle and graceful is the girl,
Awake he longs for her and in his dreams.

Picture of Odes Of Bin (part), painted by Ma Hezhi in the Song Dynasty. *Odes Of Bin – July* is a poem on agriculture, describing the scene of farmers laboring all the year round and the joy of farmers feasting together in the slack season.

When the courtship has failed,
Awake he thinks of her and in his dreams.
Filled with sorrowful thoughts,
He tosses about unable to sleep.
Short and long the floating water plants,
Left and right you may gather them.
Gentle and graceful is the girl,
He'd like to wed her, the qin and se playing.
Short and long the floating water plants,
Left and right you may collect them.
Gentle and graceful is the girl,
He'd like to marry her, bells and drums beating.

As a folk love song, it not only manifests beautiful love in the world, but also describes the beautiful course of pursuing love. This plain, refreshing, lively and refined poem full of love has been handed down from generation to generation for thousands of years with far-reaching influence. Poems in *The Book of Songs* such as *Sandalwood Felling*, *Big Rat*, *The Reeds and Rushes*, *July* and *Picking Fern-shoots* reflect bottom-class people's hard labor and spirit of resistance, depict tragic wars of resistance against foreign enemies, or express exceedingly sad and sentimental feelings. "Thick grow the rush leaves; their white dew turns to frost. He whom I love must be somewhere along this stream." "When I left here, willows shed tear. I come back now, snow bends the bough." These are all famous lines from them handed down for thousands of years.

The Book of Songs has its salient artistic characteristics. In view of the most basic forms of expression, most texts in *The Book of Songs* consist of four-character sentences, and each sentence has two beats constituting the rhythm. This simple and clear form facilitated singing and spreading, and this plain artistic form of *The Book of Songs* directly influenced the plain style of Chinese poetry. Of course, all texts in *The Book of Songs* can be sung with music, thus also manifesting a strong sense of musical beauty. Tautology, alliteration, assonance, repetition, lingering charm and the use of many function words not only constitute abundant and lifelike poetic imaginations, but also show strong musical appeal.

Picture Scroll of Proceeding with Carriage, painted by Ma Hezhi in the Song Dynasty. *Proceeding with Carriage* is a poem in *Minor Odes of the Kingdom – Decade of Lu Ming* depicting the scene of the Zhou Dynasty's army returning in triumph.

Another characteristic of *The Book of Songs* is that true feelings are expressed directly. Many texts not only truly reflect real life of that period and express authors' thoughts and feelings naturally and straightforwardly, but also have no affected form or artificial modality. Everything is a reflection of life itself. Whether written by ordinary people or higher-class scholars, they were not created on purpose. Reality leads to a high degree of integration of the ideological connotations and artistic charm of *The Book of Songs*. This style of *The Book of Songs* also exerted far-reaching influence on poetry styles in later ages.

Another important characteristic of *The Book of Songs* is, just like Confucius said, "The Odes serve to stimulate the mind. They may be used for purposes of self-contemplation. They teach the art of sociability. They show how to regulate feelings of resentment. From them you learn the more immediate duty of serving one's father, and the remoter one of serving one's prince. From them we become largely acquainted with the names of birds, beasts, and plants." The first four sentences summarize multiple aspects of the value of *The Book of Songs* such as artistic inspiration, understanding, educational functions, satire and criticism. These aspects of the value of *The Book of Songs* as China's earliest collection of poems undoubtedly exerted tremendous influence on Chinese poetry creation in later ages and even the entire Chinese literature's pursuit of aesthetic value and ideological content.

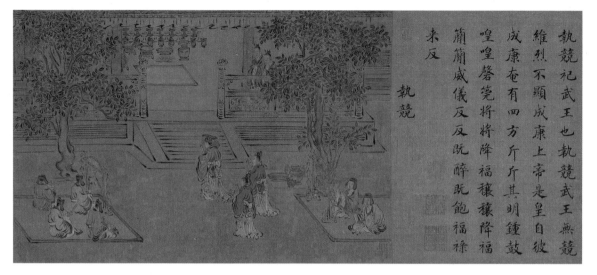

Picture of Sacrificial Odes of Zhou – Decade of Qing Miao (part), written by Emperor Gaozong of the Song Dynasty Zhao Gou and painted by Ma Hezhi. *Sacrificial Odes of Zhou – Decade of Qing Miao* consists of a total of ten poems, which are all songs for offering sacrifices to past emperors of the Zhou Dynasty.

What deserves special attention is that later people revealed artistic expression methods of ancient Chinese poetry with universal significance, i.e. description, metaphor and analogy, from the creation of *The Book of Songs*. Description refers to elaboration and parallelism; metaphor refers to comparison; analogy refers to expressing emotions through describing concrete objects and then introducing the things, thoughts and feelings that the poet wants to express through association. These three methods have different functions and characteristics but integrate with each other and interact as both cause and effect. Description, metaphor and analogy in *The Book of Songs* deeply influenced creation of poems and essays in later dynasties. It can be said that *The Book of Songs* aroused the passion for and interest in Chinese poetry creation, and nourished generations of poets.

Qu Yuan: Romantic Lyric Poems

Qu Yuan (340 BC–278 BC) was a great romantic poet in the history of Chinese ancient literature. His pioneering romantic and emotional style exerted far-reaching influence on the creation and development of Chinese poetry in later ages. Qu Yuan, with the given name of Ping and the courtesy name of Yuan, lived in the Chu State in the late Warring States Period. He was the founder of verses of Chu and the most accomplished representative writer of verses of Chu. His main representative works include *Sorrow at Parting*, *Heavenly Questions*, *Evocation*, *Nine Elegies*, *Nine Songs*, etc.

The Chu State in the Yangtze River and Han River basin was prosperous in the Spring and Autumn Period, and the Chu culture was gradually formed in long-term cultural exchange and integration with the Central Plains area in the Yellow River basin. Different from the Central Plains culture, the Chu culture had its salient and unique characteristics. "Verses of Chu," i.e. songs of the Chu State, are a new genre of poetry that emerged in the Chu State in the late Warring States Period. Different from *The Book of Songs* with realistic characteristics, "verses of Chu" have strong romantic charm and distinctive local features.

Verses of Chu (Ming block-printed edition). In the Western Han Dynasty, Liu Xiang compiled all works of Qu Yuan and works of Song Yu and others into a collection entitled Verses of Chu.

Picture of Qu Yuan Singing while Walking, painted by contemporary Fu Baoshi. In the picture, Qu Yuan banished by the imperial court is singing while walking along the Miluo River slowly with a double-edged sword at his belt.

    Sorrow at Parting is Qu Yuan's most influential representative work and a symbolic work representing the highest ideological and artistic level among verses of Chu. Qu Yuan wrote *Sorrow at Parting* against a special historical background. In the Warring States Period, the seven states contended for hegemony, and the competition between the Qin State and the Chu State was especially fierce. However, in the times of Qu Yuan, though the Chu State was still a big state, there were internal disturbances and signs of decline. Qu Yuan full of patriotic passion advocated resistance against the Qin State for salvation actively, but unfortunately he was framed by crafty sycophants for his right opinion and was scolded by the fatuous and self-indulgent King Huai of Chu. Qu Yuan's enthusiasm was in vain, but he was always worried about the Chu State and loyal to King Huai. In the face of the dark reality of unrealizable ideals, Qu Yuan sang loudly without restraint, expressed feelings in poems, and voiced good wishes such as orientation towards people, recommendation of worthy and able people, clean politics, rule of law and unification of the country. This is the reason why in *Records of the Grand Historian – Biography of Qu Yuan* Sima Qian said, "Qu Yuan wrote *Sorrow at Parting* in meditation." This shows that *Sorrow at Parting* is not a purely literary work. First of all, it demonstrates Qu Yuan's lofty political ideals, epitomizes his patriotic passion, and reflects his glorious, noble and righteous character.

Sorrow at Parting fully manifests Qu Yuan's glorious ideological character. With a length of about 2,500 Chinese characters, *Sorrow at Parting* is not a narrative poem but a lyric poem expressing the poet's own feelings based on the poet's ideological character. There are two highlights of Qu Yuan's ideological character. The first one is his deep and persistent patriotic passion. Qu Yuan always deeply and wholeheartedly loved his motherland in deep distress, and his ideals of "revitalization of the state under the king's rule" and "benevolent governance" both originated from his patriotic passion. He did not give any thought to his advancement and even his life. Sycophants framed him, King Huai ignored him, and the Chu State expelled him. All these could not change his resolute patriotic faith! The second one is his unremitting pursuit of truth and his spirit of ruthless criticism of the dark reality. Lu Xun praised Qu Yuan for expressing feelings directly and "saying what people dared not say in the past" in *Sorrow at Parting*. Qu Yuan pursued truth without regret even at the cost of his life. "Long, long had been my road and far, far was the journey: I would go up and down to seek my heart's desire." Qu Yuan understood the dark reality of the Chu State and the ingrained common customs hard to overcome; he was aware of the perilous state of the country and the sufferings of the people; he knew how fatuous and self-indulgent King Huai of Chu was and how shameless sycophants were quite well. He ruthlessly exposed and criticized all these in *Sorrow at Parting*. What is even more precious is the persistent spirit of doing something even

God and Goddess of the Xiang River, painted by Wen Zhengming in the Ming Dynasty. *God of the Xiang River and Goddess of the Xiang River* in *Nine Songs* by Qu Yuan show the love and yearning between the god and goddess of the Xiang River and the sad impossibility of their convergence.

though it is impossible visible from Qu Yuan and *Sorrow at Parting*. As a result, Qu Yuan and his *Sorrow at Parting* showed more clearly the "independent and unswerving" magnetic personality and the power of thought.

Sorrow at Parting also shows unique artistic charm. It is the longest lyric poem in the history of Chinese ancient literature and the first long lyric poem created self-consciously and independently.

In terms of methods of expressing emotions, *Sorrow at Parting* established the status and role of poetry as the main expressive genre, representing the beginning of romanticism in the history of Chinese literature. *Sorrow at Parting* and *The Book of Songs* became two origins of Chinese realistic and romantic literature. In fact *Sorrow at Parting* fully shapes the lyric protagonist's image, and the poet's family background, life, ideals, pursuits and the painstaking efforts made to realize these ideals are all shown through the protagonist's expression of emotions. *Sorrow at Parting* seems highly integrated because of the poet's high degree of emotional consciousness. Meanwhile, in comparison with *The Book of Songs*, *Sorrow at Parting* features new improvement on the basis of the expression methods of description, metaphor and analogy, especially with respect to expression of emotions through describing concrete objects, blending of feelings and settings, integration of subjectivity and objectivity, etc., free association and boundless imagination. Colorful images and artistic conceptions are created in a highly poetic atmosphere, showing the magic charm of romanticism.

In terms of poetry forms, *Sorrow at Parting* breaks from the four-character form of *The Book of Songs* and forms a vigorous and unconstrained style not limited to one pattern. Literary critic of the Qing Dynasty Liu Xizai (1813–1881) sighed that *Sorrow at Parting* "contains unrelated sentences full of structural and tonal changes; however, something does not change of course." Though *Sorrow at Parting* is a poem, prose writing methods are used a lot. This style featuring free structures, combination of prose and rhymes and many grammatical changes was called "sorrow style" in later ages. This is a major contribution of Qu Yuan and *Sorrow at Parting* to Chinese literature.

Besides, *Sorrow at Parting* also has strong and prominent local features. It "records the language, sounds, places and things of the Chu State," describing social customs particular to the Chu State, transcribing the dialects and local expressions of the Chu State, and leaving a precious historical scroll about the Chu State to later people.

Tao Yuanming: A Hermit's Pastoral Poems

Tao Yuanming (c. 365–427) was the greatest Chinese hermit poet, and his pastoral poems occupy a glorious place in the history of Chinese poetry. Tao Yuanming, with the courtesy name of Yuanliang, the given name of Qian, the alternative courtesy name of Yuanming and the alias of Mr. Wuliu, was born in a declining bureaucratic family. His father died early, but his family's poverty did not affect his determination to study hard. He read all kinds of books from Confucian classics to various "heterodox books." In his early years, he aspired to benefit people in the world but deeply loved nature and detested fame, fortune and secularity. The thoughts of Laozi and Zhuangzi influenced him deeply. From the age of 29, to make a living, he served as a low-level official (something like a magistrate). In the next 13 years, his official career was rough, and he served as an official sometimes and lived in seclusion sometimes. At the age of 41, unwilling to "bend the back

Asking a Wayfarer What Road Lies Ahead, painted by Ma Shi in the Ming Dynasty, depicts the scene of Tao Yuanming returning to his hometown after his resignation and asking a wayfarer which way to go at a crossroad.

for five bushels of rice," he finally resigned from his official post in anger, returned to his hometown Chaisang, became a hermit and tilled fields personally. In the next 22 years before his death, Tao Yuanming never came out from the mountains to become an official. He was contented in poverty and devoted to things spiritual, wrote poems, drank wine, and farmed and read books for self-amusement, showing his tranquil and noble state of mind.

Tao Yuanming's seclusion was of important and peculiar significance in the history of Chinese literature. First, Tao Yuanming's resignation from his official post and seclusion truly revealed his real personality, showed his thorough understanding of the dark side of the society, the dirty officialdom and life values, and manifested the poet's unique state of life and peculiar understanding of art. All people in the world deem *Ah, homeward bound I go* as Tao Yuanming's expression of his true feelings about seclusion:

Picture of Yuanming's Drunken Return, painted by Zhang Peng in the Ming Dynasty, shows Tao Yuanming's bearing of a hermit drinking wine beside chrysanthemums.

> *Ah, homeward bound I go! Why not go home, seeing that my field and gardens are overgrown? Myself have made my soul serf to my body: why have vain regrets and mourn alone? Fret not over bygones and the forward journey take. Only a short distance have I gone astray, and I know today I am right, if yesterday was a complete mistake. Lightly floats and drifts the boat, and*

the wind gently flows and flaps my gown. I inquire the road of a wayfarer, and sulk at the dimness of the dawn.

Here, Tao Yuanming clearly revealed his determination to leave officialdom and never make "my soul serf to my body." He wanted to live free and indulged in imagining how free and happy he would become after leaving officialdom and returning to the countryside! *Ah, homeward bound I go* is not a real description of the life of Tao Yuanming as a recluse but a description of how he felt when he had just decided to become a hermit and his aspiration to future life. Though this article is short, it has the style and beauty of metrical composition and is plain like all other poems by Tao Yuanming.

Secondly, Tao Yuanming's seclusion itself had special connotations. Tao's seclusion was not a strategy. He really became a hermit and realized his life values in seclusion. Therefore, after becoming a hermit, he never wanted to become an official again and devoted himself to rural life wholeheartedly. People said that Tao Yuanming kindly communicated with farmers as their equal. Actually he had completely turned himself into a farmer. He did farm work and tilled land himself, not only suffering hardships, but also tasting the sweet. He laid a foundation for rural life through his labor and enjoyed unparalleled joy of life in this course. This is shown in the first of *Five Poems of Returning to the Life of Farmers*:

I've loathed the madding crowd since I was a boy
While hills and mountains have filled me with joy.
By mistake I sought mundane careers
And got entrapped in them for thirty years.
Birds in the cage would long for wooded hills;
Fish in the pond would yearn for flowing rills.
So I reclaim the land in southern fields
To suit my bent for reaping farmland yields.
My farm contains a dozen mu of ground;
My cottage has eight or nine rooms around.
The elm and willow cover backside eaves

While peach and plum trees shade my yard with leaves.
The distant village dimly looms somewhere,
With smoke from chimneys drifting in the air.
In silent country lanes a stray dog barks;
Amid the mulberry trees cocks crow with larks.
My house is free from worldly moil or gloom
While ease and quiet permeate my private room.
When I escape from bitter strife with men,
I live a free and easy life again.

This poem truly portrays the happy mood and tranquil life after the poet's return to the countryside. After reflecting on his "entry into the secular world by mistake" 30 years before, the poet described his contentment and amusement in the countryside, the farm, cottage, the elm and willow, peach and plum trees, a barking dog and crowing cocks in natural and harmonious scene in detail. Of course, more importantly, people can feel how pure and happy the poet's state of mind was.

We should also see that though Tao Yuanming returned to nature and the countryside, his state of mind could not be as calm as stagnant water. The most beautiful landscape could not possibly sever the ties between the poet and the outside world. The second of his *Miscellaneous Poems* is as follows:

The white sun has sunk behind the west peaks,
The pale moon arises from the east ranges.
Vast luminance spreads over myriad leagues:
What a view in the expanse of the blank heavens!
Wind comes in through casements and entrance,
My pillow and mattress in night's middle turn cold.
Weather changes and I realize the season's different,
Sleepless, I realize how endless is the night!
I'm about to speak but there's no one to respond,
Brandishing the cup I invite my shadow to drink.

Suns and moons have cast me aside,
My lofty ambition hasn't been fulfilled.
At the thought of this I feel sad,
Restless the whole night through.

Tao Yuanming was a broad-minded person of ideals and integrity after all. He became a hermit to realize his life values but often thought about the outside world. The most tranquil life could not conceal the restlessness in the poet's heart, so "at the thought of this I feel sad, restless the whole night through"! This shows that Tao Yuanming's seclusion had abundant connotations. There was aspiration in disappointment, the wish to go far in joy and restlessness in tranquility. All these jointly constituted Tao Yuanming's broad mind, feelings and aspirations in reclusive rural life.

Tao Yuanming's pastoral poems formed its unique artistic characteristics. In terms of the overall style, Tao Yuanming's pastoral poems express his attitude towards nature with unique circumstances and modes, elaborate the aesthetic relationship between man and nature, and demonstrate the beauty of harmonious coexistence of man and nature with an elegant and indifferent sentiment. The fifth poem in his *Drinking* is famous and widely known:

Building me a hut in the human realm,
But I'm free from the clamor of horses and carriages.
How comes it to be so?
If my heart is aloof, my dwelling will be remote.
I gather chrysanthemums by my eastern hedge,
Can vaguely see the southern hills.
Mountain air is balmy at dusk,
Birds fly back one after another.
This scenery contains the true:
I forget what I was going to say before I even argue.

Walk Home with the Moon Shouldering the Hoe, painted by Shi Tao in the Qing Dynasty, is based on the poetic sentiment of Tao Yuanming's *Third Poem of Returning to the Life of Farmers*: "At dawn, I rise and go out to weed the field; shouldering the hoe, I walk home with the moon."

This is not just admiration of beautiful natural scenery or the poet's infatuation with the leisurely mood, but reaches the state of philosophy and the state of unity of man and nature and integration of things and himself.

Most of Tao Yuanming's pastoral poems with fresh and plain words depict rural life and give people a sense of reality. Many pastoral scenes depicted by the poet are familiar to people, e.g. the third one of his *Five Poems of Returning to the Life of Farmers*:

> *Under the southern hill I grow the pea and bean,*
> *For the weeds the tender shoots are sparse and lean.*
> *With the sun I rise the weeds to remove,*
> *In moonlight, shouldering a hoe, I homeward move.*
> *The narrow path is overgrown with long grass,*
> *The evening dews wet my clothes as I pass.*
> *I'm not so much worried about my attire,*
> *As being unable to follow my cherished desire.*

Everything is from very common daily life but contains the poet's life ideals. Without any preaching or long argumentation, it seems like muttering, easy to understand, natural, plain and pure. This is just a manifestation of the plural value of Tao Yuanming's reclusive life, charisma and literary style.

Poet Immortal Li Bai

The poems of Li Bai (701–762) represent another peak of romanticism in the history of Chinese ancient poetry after Qu Yuan. His unrestrained personality, excellent ability and profound ingenious thoughts pushed creation of Chinese romantic poems to a new height.

Li Bai, with the courtesy name of Taibai, was a native of Chengji, Longxi (today's Tianshui, Gansu). His ancestors migrated to Suiye City in Central Asia at the end of the Sui Dynasty, and Li Bai was born there. Later, he migrated to Qinglian village, Zhangming County, Mianzhou, Sichuan (today's Jiangyou County, Sichuan) with his father, hence his alias Qinglian Jushi. When Li Bai studied, practiced sword play and wandered in his early years, he began to write poems. Though poems such as *The Moon over Mount Brow* and *Song for White Hair* are not outstanding, they show his romantic and transcendental style. When Li Bai was young, he wandered around, broadened his vision and wrote more and more poems. Famous works such as *River Chant*, *A Song of Changgan*, *Viewing the Waterfall at Mount Lu*, *Bidding a Friend Farewell at Jingmen Ferry* and *Seeing off Meng Haoran at Tower of Yellow Crane* also emerged successively. In the Tianbao Period, he became a member of the Imperial Academy and was treated with courtesy by Emperor Xuanzong of the Tang Dynasty, but he was

Picture of Drunken Taibai, painted by Su Liupeng in the Qing Dynasty, depicts the scene of Li Bai supported and served by two eunuchs in the palace of Emperor Xuanzong of the Tang Dynasty after getting drunk.

soon repulsed by influential officials and resigned. Later, after social disturbances such as the An-Shi Rebellion, he suffered bad luck and frustration, wandered around, and at last died in Dangtu, Anhui away from his hometown. After leaving Chang'an, Li Bai wrote famous works full of his deep thought and inspiration such as 59 poems in *Verses in the Old Style*, *The Hard Road*, *Hard Ways to Shu*, *Bring in the Wine* and *Tianmu Mountain Ascended in a Dream*. More than 990 poems and essays written by Li Bai are included in *The Complete Works of Li Taibai*.

Li Bai had complicated thoughts and an unrestrained personality. The orthodox rite and morality of the Confucian School, the transcendence and seclusion of the Taoist School, the unruliness of the School of Diplomacy and the thoughts of knights-errant wandering among mountains and rivers and missing nothing were all manifested by him, but generally speaking, Li Bai had his unique thought and temperament, the most prominent aspect being the conflict between ideals and reality: he had a sense of responsibility for the state and society and strongly wished to go into the society, but meanwhile he was quite unsatisfied and angry about the rulers' dissolution and the dark side of the society; he hoped he could do something but was out of tune with the powerful and influential people and the hierarchy. He always hoped to realize the great wish to "benefit people in the world," "stabilize the state" and then retire after successful accomplishment of his tasks to make his life complete under the emperor's favor. Obviously, this thought of his was too naïve, and the ruthless reality crushed his dream time and again. Such experiences full of conflict and pain, on the one hand, strengthened Li Bai's independent, unruly, arrogant and unrestrained ideological character and, on the other hand, also directly influenced the formation of the romantic style in his poetry creation.

Li Bai's artistic accomplishments in poetry are epitomized in three aspects. The first is the unrestrained momentum: "From both sides of the River thrust out the cliffs blue; leaving the sun behind, a lonely sail comes forth." in *Mount Heaven's Gate Viewed from Afar*, "Its torrent dashes down three thousand feet from high; as if the Silver River fell from azure sky." in *Viewing the Waterfall at Mount Lu*, "As the riverbanks echo still with the monkey's cry aloud. Before a myriad mountains the swift boat has glided away." in *Leaving Baidi Town in Early Morning*, and "I will mount a long wind some day and break the heavy waves and set my cloudy sail straight and bridge the deep, deep sea." in *The Hard Road…* These thrilling lines transcending time and space without parallel in history all show the poet's extraordinary and outstanding momentum.

The second is romantic charm. The widely known poem *Bring in the Wine* fully displays the poet's romantic feelings without regard to the past and future:

See how the Yellow River's waters move out of heaven.
Entering the ocean, never to return.
See how lovely locks in bright mirrors in high chambers,
Though silken-black at morning, have changed by night to snow.
Oh, let a man of spirit venture where he pleases
And never tip his golden cup empty toward the moon!
Since heaven gave the talent, let it be employed!
Spin a thousand pieces of silver, all of them come back!
Cook a sheep, kill a cow, whet the appetite,
And make me, of three hundred bowls, one long drink!
To the old master, Cen,
And the young scholar, Danqiu,
Bring in the wine!
Let your cups never rest!
Let me sing you a song!
Let your ears attend!
What are bell and drum, rare dishes and treasure?
Let me be forever drunk and never come to reason!
Sober men of olden days and sages are forgotten,
And only the great drinkers are famous for all time.
Prince Chen paid at a banquet in the Palace of Perfection
Ten thousand coins for a cask of wine, with many a laugh and quip.
Why say, my host, that your money is gone?
Go and buy wine and we'll drink it together!
My flower-dappled horse,

Picture of the Waterfall at Mount Lu, painted by Xie Shichen in the Ming Dynasty, is based on the poetic sentiment of Li Bai's *Viewing the Waterfall at Mount Lu*.

My furs worth a thousand,
Hand them to the boy to exchange for good wine,
And we'll drown away the woes of ten thousand generations!

This poem is forthright, forceful, extremely romantic and passionate. After reading this poem by Li Bai, everybody can see through the vanity of life and the world!

The third is the enchanting poetic feeling. Many poems by Li Bai are enchanting, colorful and deeply emotional, such as *Sitting Alone in Jingting Mountain*:

Flocks of birds fly high and vanish;
A single cloud, alone, calmly drifts on.
Never tired of looking at each other –
Only the Jingting Mountain and me.

To Wang Lun is also full of emotion:

I'm on board; we're about to sail,
When there's stamping and singing on shore;
Peach Blossom Pool is a thousand feet deep,
Yet not so deep, Wang Lun, as your love for me.

Picture of Hard Ways to Shu, painted by Xie Shichen in the Ming Dynasty, vividly shows the hard ways to Shu "more rugged than the ways to heaven" in Li Bai's *Hard Ways to Shu*.

The short four-line poem is eloquent, natural and vivid, integrating acts and scenes, narration and expression of feelings, and the intangible and tangible. The writing style is easy, special and unforgettable.

Bodhisattva-like Barbarians is another example:

A flat-top forest stretches far in embroidered mist;
A cluster of mountains cool is tinged with heartbreak blue.
The mansion in creeping dusk in clad,
Someone up there is sad.
On marble steps I stand forlorn.
Birds fly hurriedly by back to roost.
Where, pray, is the way home?
Along a string of wayside pavilions I roam.

Picture of the poetic sentiment of *Seeing off Meng Haoran at Tower of Yellow Crane*, painted by Shi Tao in the Qing Dynasty. Meng Haoran was Li Bai's bosom friend and a poet he admired very much.

Picture of the poetic sentiment of *A Tranquil Night*, painted by Shi Tao in the Qing Dynasty. *A Tranquil Night* is one of the most widely spread poems by Li Bai, expressing a traveler's nostalgia.

People on a journey are often stirred by sights and miss their close relatives anytime and anywhere, but this poem is special in that deep and honest affection, naturalness and indifference combine both the real and unreal. The last two lines, especially the last line "along a string of wayside pavilions I roam" consisting of five Chinese characters, fully express the poet's true feelings and boundless melancholy during his journey.

Li Bai's poems are diversified in thought and art. His unparalleled imagination and creativity refreshed and invigorated the style of Chinese poetry that had remained unchanged for hundreds of years. His contemporary and great poet Du Fu highly praised Li Bai's poetry, "The poems of Po are unequalled. His thoughts are never categorical, but fly high in the wind." "When the pen is to paper, the wind and rain have been shocked, and when the poetry is finished, even the ghosts and spirits have been touched by it." Another contemporary poet He Zhizhang (659–744) praised Li Bai as a "banished immortal" from heaven when they first met, so later people called Li Bai "Poet Immortal."

Poet Sage Du Fu

Realism is the profoundest and longest tradition of Chinese poetry. In the Tang Dynasty, Du Fu (712–770) made this tradition shine like never before. Du Fu's poetry, with his real feelings, close observations and gloomy and sincere emotions, reflects almost all major social and political events from the late Tianbao Period of the Tang Dynasty to the Dali Period, especially the great traumas caused by the turbulent times to people's livelihood, expresses his closest concern, and shows his indignation unequivocally. In terms of poetic art, Du Fu represented the greatest previous accomplishments, stood at a new height of the times, inherited from predecessors, inspired those who came later, achieved mastery through comprehensive studies, and created a unique style. In the history of Chinese literature, Du Fu's poetry deserved to be called "poetic history" and "poet sage." Now more than 1,400 poems by Du Fu exist. *Collected Works of Du Fu with Notes* by Chou Zhaoao (1638–1717), a scholar who lived in the late Ming Dynasty and early Qing Dynasty, is a detailed variorum existing today.

Figure of Du Fu, painted by contemporary Jiang Zhaohe

Du Fu, with the courtesy name of Zimei, called himself "Du Ling the Commoner" and was often called "Du Shaoling." In his late years, he worked as an acting councilor at the Ministry of Works temporarily; therefore, later people called him "Du of the Ministry of Works." When he was young, Du Fu studied hard, began his grant tour of more than ten years at the age of 20, greatly broadened his vision, and accumulated abundant life experience. When he was high-spirited and had bright prospects in his middle age, Du Fu cherished the political ideal of "helping the monarch surpass Yao and Shun and renewing the glorious customs" in vain, lived with difficulties in Chang'an for ten years, could not dedicate himself to the service of his country, and could not advance. The difficulties in life made Du Fu determined to express his thoughts with poems, write down his worries about his country and people and realize great ambitions and strategies. In this period, he wrote famous poems such as *Soldiers' Song*, *A Song of Fair Women* and *Expressing Feelings in Five Hundred Words on the Way to Fengxian County from the Capital*, and their characteristic of "poetic history" was increasingly clear. The An-Shi Rebellion that broke out in 755 caused great traumas to the society, and brought deeper distress and grief to Du Fu. He fled from calamities, avoided disasters, had no permanent residence, and wandered from place to place. Painful experiences let him get closer to people at the bottom and social reality and see through the society more clearly. Many of his classic poems such as "Three Officials," "Three Departures," *Qiang Village*, *A Spring View*, *Washing Weapons and Horses* and *The Northward March* were all written in this period. From 759 to his death, Du Fu always wandered in the southwest. In this period, Du Fu's poetic thought was gloomier, and his art was more sophisticated. His early poems were mostly archaic Yuefu poems, but in this period he obviously wrote more seven-character metrical poems and made major accomplishments. *My Thatched Hut Wrecked by the Autumn Wind*, *On Hearing Government Troops Recapture Henan and Hebei*, *The Temple of the Premier of Shu*, *Climbing the Height* and the eight poems in *Autumn Meditations* are all important representative poems created Du Fu in the late period.

The poems created by Du Fu, the most famous realistic poet in the history of Chinese literature, show important and unique ideological characteristics and artistic features.

First, his poems express abundant thoughts, profound views and sharp criticisms. Du Fu was a very ambitious poet. The poem *Gazing on Mount Tai* written by him in his early years shows the poet's broad vision and the width of his mind:

O peak of peaks, how high it stands!
One boundless green o'er spreads two States.
A marvel done by Nature's hands,
O'er light and shade it dominates.
Clouds rise therefrom and lave my breast;
My eyes are strained to see birds fleet.
Try to ascend the mountain's crest:
It dwarfs all peaks under our feet.

Soldiers' Song (part), painted by contemporary Xu Yansun. *Soldiers' Song* is a Yuefu poem deeply manifesting the great disaster caused to the people by years of warfare and the people's hatred of war.

The poem's momentum is tremendous! Abundant experience of departures and disturbances, worries about the country and love for people constitute the basis of Du Fu's life and the keynote of his thoughts. "All the years I worried about people" and "I'm willing to dedicate my life to benefit people" fully reflects Du Fu's spirit of actively going into the society, helping rescue the country willingly and pleading in the name of the people, so later people praised him: "All poems written by Shaoling show his worries about the country!" Besides, Du Fu also truly recorded the society and history of that period with his poems, which can be called "poetic history." "Three Officials," "Three Departures," *My Thatched Hut Wrecked by the Autumn Wind*, *On Hearing Government Troops Recapture Henan and Hebei* and the eight poems in *Autumn Meditations* all depict real scenes of social life, expose the dark side of the society, and criticize rulers' dissolution and fatuity. Every sigh of the poet originated from his personal experience of real life.

Second, Du Fu's poems have their own style, manifesting the power of the poet's personality, firm writing style and unbending will. His famous poem *Spring View* is one example.

Though a country be sundered, hills and rivers endure;
And spring comes green again to trees and grasses
Where petals have been shed like tears
And lonely birds have sung their grief.
After the war-fires of three months,
One message from home is worth a ton of gold.
I stroke my white hair. It has grown too thin
To hold the hairpins any more.

Here there are mountains, rivers, grasses, trees, flowers and birds, but the whole poem expresses the poet's grief and indignation about the political situation. The last two lines in particular show the poet's anxious and painful state very vividly. *The Temple of the Premier of Shu* is another example:

The thatched cottage Du Fu lived in while staying in Chengdu. Here he wrote *My Thatched Hut Wrecked by the Autumn Wind*, shouting at the top of his voice, "If I could get a mansion with a thousand, ten thousand rooms, a great shelter for all the world's scholars, together in joy!"

Where is the temple of the famous Premier?
In a deep pine grove near the City of Silk,
With the green grass of spring coloring the steps,
And birds chirping happily under the leaves.
The third summons weighted him with affairs of state
And to two generations he gave his true heart,
But before he could conquer, he was dead;
And heroes have wept on their coats ever since.

The An-Shi Rebellion caused endless disasters. The poet visited the temple of Zhuge Liang in Chengdu, pondered on the past, wrote a poem to express his feelings, and sighed with infinite regret. Fortunately, he was not destroyed by the darkness in front of him or immersed in historical grief, but motivated by his feelings and inspired in gloom.

Third, Du Fu's poems are voluminous and have diverse styles. Du Fu's early poems are mostly five-character archaic poems, and his later poems are mostly seven-character metrical poems. The five-character poems of varying lengths and styles are natural, smooth and not limited to one type, including neat short poems such as *Gazing on Mount Tai*, *Moonlit Night* and *Spring View* and long poems such as *Expressing Feelings in Five Hundred Words*, The Northward March, "Three Officials" and "Three Departures;" the seven-character poems also include metrical poems featuring rigorous structures, strict antitheses and harmonious rhymes and the so-called irregular works such as *My Thatched Hut Wrecked by the Autumn Wind* and *Washing Weapons and Horses*, showing indulgence in neatness and rhymes in unrestraint and fully demonstrating the bearing of a master. Du Fu both narrated and expressed emotions. His scenery description was also outstanding. *Climbing the Height* is an example:

The wind so swift, the sky so deep, sad gibbons cry;
Water so clear and sand so white, backward birds fly;
The boundless forest sheds its leaves shower by shower;
The boundless river rolls its waves hour after hour.
Far from home in autumn, I'm grieved to see my plight;
After my long illness, I climb alone this height,
Living in hard times, at my frosted hair I pine;
Pressed by poverty, I give up my cup of wine.

Looking far at the height and looking down from above, the poet could see various scenes in picturesque disorder in front of him. As the scenes changed, the feelings expressed by the poet also kept pulsating. The whole poem is gloomy and cadent, and can manifest the style of Du Fu's poems very well. "The boundless forest sheds its leaves shower by shower; the boundless river rolls its waves hour after hour" can be called natural lines blending feelings and settings. Later people highly praised this poem as not only the best seven-character metrical poem of the Tang Dynasty, but also the best seven-character metrical poem of all times!

Du Fu's poems are plain but full of ups and downs, lasting forever as the high mountains and long rivers and describing stunning love and hate. Most of them are magnificent and gloomy sentimental poems representing the fascinating peak of poetic perfection!

Bai Juyi and "New Yuefu"

Bai Juyi (772–846) was another great realist poet of the Tang Dynasty. His outstanding contributions lied in not only his excellent poetry creation, but also his proposal of a series of theories on realistic poetry through advocating the New Yuefu Movement. All these exerted major far-reaching influence on that period and later ages.

Bai Juyi, with the courtesy name of Letian and the alias of Xiangshan Jushi, was a native of Taiyuan born in Xinzheng, Henan (today's Xinzheng County, Henan Province). In his youth, he wandered in the area between the Yangtze River and Huaihe River, studied hard later, and served as Reminder of the Left, Left Grand Master Admonisher, etc. His official career was not smooth in his middle age. He was framed by political opponents and was demoted to the post of Military Governor of Jiang Prefecture. In his late years, he lived in Luoyang idly until his death. This shows that Bai Juyi's life experience was a course of changing from aspiration and determination to depression and despondency, but he was concerned about people's sufferings. "Aspiring to benefit all people and maintaining personal integrity in action" is his main ideological tendency.

Bai Yuji was the most prolific poet among the poets of the Tang Dynasty. Now nearly 3,000 poems created by him exist, collected in *Bai's Changqing Collection*. Bai Juyi classified more than 1,300 poems he wrote before the age of 51 into four categories: "satirical poems, leisure poems, sentimental poems and unregulated verses." Among them, the most influential ones are his satirical poems represented by the 50 new Yuefu poems and ten poems in Songs of *Internal Regions of Qin*. Besides, his sentimental and melancholy poems such as *The Eternal Regret* and *Songs of the Lute* are all famous classic poems.

Bai Juyi was an advocate of the New Yuefu Poetry Movement, and the concept of "New Yuefu" was first proposed by Bai Juyi. New Yuefu is Yuefu-style poetry on new themes and current events,

Picture of Songs of the Lute, painted by Guo Xu in the Ming Dynasty. Above the picture is the whole poem of *Songs of the Lute* written in cursive script, and below the picture is the scene of the encounter of the poet Bai Juyi and the female lute player, highlighting the poem's theme, "We are both ill-starred, drifting on the face of the earth."

including three aspects. The first is original new themes. The so-called new themes are mainly relative to ancient themes borrowed for most old Yuefu poems. New Yuefu poems have new themes, so they are also called "new-theme Yuefu poems." The second is comments on current events, continuing the realistic style of poetry pioneered by Du Fu. New Yuefu poems give more emphasis to satire and criticism. The third is that though new Yuefu poems are called "Yuefu," not all of them can be sung with music.

The reason why Bai Juyi advocated the New Yuefu Poetry Movement was closely related to his poetry theories and ideals. First, Bai Juyi emphasized in *Preface to New Yuefu* from the very beginning: poems "should be created for the emperor, ministers, people, objects and events." He always stuck to the principle of "writing articles for the times and writing poems for events." Bai Juyi's view on poetry is very simple and clear, centering on "people," i.e. reflecting people's sufferings. He clearly proposed the thought and slogan of poetry for people like never before. It was of very important realistic significance in that period. Secondly, Bai Juyi proposed that poetry should "supervise the political situation" and "release people's emotions." In other words, poetry as literature must interact with social politics and must communicate with people's feelings. Literature is always about "thoughts on events" and "emotions," and is not just a kind of entertainment. Therefore, literature and poetry have the unique function and characteristic of combining education with recreation. Third, Bai Juyi advocated that the contents and forms of poetry should be highly unified, with emphasis on the former and that forms should not be polished deliberately because simple and plain forms were acceptable as long as they were closely related to contents.

These theories advocated by Bai Juyi played an active and important role in the development of Chinese ancient poetry and the whole

After Bath, a picture painted by Li Yu in the Qing Dynasty, is based on the poetic sentiment of Bai Juyi's *The Eternal Regret*, which describes the tragic love between Emperor Xuanzong of the Tang Dynasty and Imperial Consort Yang.

literature. Under the influence and push of Bai Juyi, a number of advocates of new Yuefu jointly promoted the development and expansion of the New Yuefu Poetry Movement and left an important chapter in the history of Chinese poetry.

Bai Juyi not only advocated the New Yuefu Movement, but also earnestly practiced what one advocated and pushed forward the development of new Yuefu with his creation and practice. There are many moving poems among the 50 poems in *New Yuefu* such as *The White-haired Palace Maid*, *The Old Man with the Broken Arm*, *The Old Man of Duling* and *The Old Charcoal Seller*, not only truly reproducing the social life scenes of that period, but also revealing his thorough understanding of life. "Silent, she sees the birds appear and disappear,and counts nor spring nor autumn coming year by year," "A ghost, I'd have wandered in Yunnan, always looking for home, over the graves of ten thousand soldiers, mournfully hovering" and "Though his coat is thin, he hopes winter will set in, for cold weather will keep up the charcoal's good price" are all deeply moving lines, containing incisive criticisms of the society and filling people with awe. Many long Yuefu poems by Bai Juyi include such easy-to-read, penetrating and meaningful lines with great depth.

Besides, Bai Juyi's long poems represented by *The Eternal Regret* are highly narrative and contain many very emotional lines in narrations such as "But rebels beat their war drums, making the earth quake and 'Song of Rainbow Skirt and Coat of Feathers' break" and "The boundless sky and endless earth may pass away, but this vow unfulfilled will be regretted for aye." These are famous lines handed down for thousands of years.

Bai Juyi's poems not only excel in narration and expression of emotions, but also depict scenery very well. *On Lake Qiantang in Spring* is one example.

West of Pavilion Jia and north of Lonely Hill,
Water brim level with the bank and clouds hang low.
Disputing for sunny trees, early orioles trill;
Pecking vernal mud in, young swallows come and go.
A riot of blooms begins to dazzle the eye;
Amid short grass the horse hoofs can barely be seen.
I love best the east of the lake under the sky;
The bank paved with white sand is shaded by willows green.

Picture of the Four Pleasures of Nan Shenglu (part), painted by Chen Hongshou in the Ming Dynasty. In the picture, an old woman stands beside Bai Juyi, showing Bai Juyi's poems are easy to understand and can even be comprehended by old women.

The enchanting air of early spring fills the spring scenery. Just like all these are very natural, the poet's style of writing is also very relaxed. There is no meticulous polishing and no purposeful exaggeration. Trilling early orioles and young swallows pecking mud enter readers' hearts naturally. *Grass on the Ancient Plain* – Farewell to a Friend, a famous poem created by Bai Juyi in his early years, is more widely known:

Wild grasses spread over ancient plain;
With spring and fall they come and go.
Fire tries to burn them up in vain;
They rise again when spring winds blow.
Their fragrance overruns the way;
Their green invades the ruined town.
To see my friend going away,
My sorrow grows like grass overgrown.

There is an interesting story behind this poem. It is said that Bai Juyi went to the capital Chang'an from the region south of the lower reaches of the Yangtze River at the age of 16 and called on Gu Kuang (727–815), a celebrated scholar of that period. After learning Bai Juyi's name (with the literal meaning of living for free easily), Gu Kuang joked by saying "Prices are high in Chang'an, and it is not easy to live here." However, when he read "Fire tries to burn them up in vain; they rise again when spring winds blow" in his book of poems, he could not help praising him, "With such talent, you can live here without any difficulty!" Thus, Bai Juyi's poetry became prominent, and he finally became a very important poet in the history of Chinese poetry.

Beautiful Ci Poetry

Ci poems as a kind of ancient Chinese poems can be sung with music. The earliest ci poems emerged among people in the Sui Dynasty. At that time, ci poems were regarded by scholars as unrefined short lyrics different from poems. In the mid Tang Dynasty, Bai Juyi and Liu Yuxi (772–842) "wrote lines according to tune beats" and created tunes such as *Recalling the South of the Yangtze River*, and many poets also wrote ci poems sometimes. Thus ci-poetry began to occupy a place in literary creation and some excellent works emerged. In the late Tang Dynasty and the Five Dynasties, literati ci poetry's position was further established, and ci specialists and collections emerged. For example, Wen Tingjun (c. 812–866) was the first ci poet to compose ci poems to given tunes. *Collection from among the Flowers* includes his 66 ci poems. 500 ci poems written by 18 ci poets are included in this earliest collection of ci poems. Thus, ci poetry became an independent genre in the history of Chinese literature and developed in parallel with poetry. In the Song Dynasty, ci poetry thrived, and famous masters emerged one after another. Great ci poets such as Su Shi and Xin Qiji contributed to the maximal improvement and development of ci poetry creation. Ci poetry of the Song Dynasty became comparable to poetry of the Tang Dynasty, and was reputed as the culmination of literature by later people.

Su Shi: Creating a New State of Ci Poetry

Small Portrait of Dongpo, painted by Zhao Mengfu in the Yuan Dynasty

Compared with poetry of the Tang Dynasty, ci poetry of the Song Dynasty is more exquisite in form and more refined in structure. Therefore, most ci poems of the Song Dynasty are skillful, meticulous, graceful and exquisite works. Su Dongpo changed the soft and mild style, and created a new fashion and pattern of ci poetry of the Song Dynasty as grand, unrestrained and magnificent as the great river flowing eastward.

Su Shi began his official career at the age of 25, served as governor of Mizhou and Hangzhou, and was demoted to be an official in Huangzhou and Huizhou. Generally speaking, Su Shi was always amid party struggles of the Northern Song Dynasty in his lifetime, made no great political accomplishment, had a mediocre official career, and felt more disappointment than exaltation.

However, Su Shi became a literary phenomenon and could be called a flag of literature in the mid Northern Song Dynasty. In terms of literary opinions, he clearly opposed the bad literary styles in the late Tang Dynasty, the Five Dynasties and the early Song Dynasty, including some new abuses brought by the Classical Prose Movement, put forward many new aesthetic views of positive significance, and made important contributions to the development of literature in the Song Dynasty.

Su Shi made outstanding achievements in poems, essays and ci poems, but his most important contribution was innovation and breakthroughs in ci poetry. Su Shi's achievements in ci poetry were higher than his achievements in poems and essays. First, Su Shi attached great importance to the literary genre of ci poetry theoretically. Though many excellent ci poems were written before Su Shi, people did not understand ci poetry correctly and were far from deeming ci poetry as a literary genre. Most people "composed ci poetry to given tunes" and deemed it as an unorthodox school of "mocking and playful" poetry. Even Ouyang Xiu called "composition of ci poetry to given tunes" as "skill of little worth." However, Su Shi held an original opinion. He clearly thought ci poetry and poetry were both literary genres of equal status. Ci poems were "poems consisting of long and short lines," and Su Shi "took poetry as ci poetry" in his creation. This view and practice of Su Shi played an important role in the establishment of ci poetry as a literary genre and the development of creation. It can be said that after Su Shi, people paid less attention to the formal differences between ci poetry and poetry, ci also became a genre of poetry in the broad sense, and ci poetry and poetry entered the field of literature as equals. This was a breakthrough of epoch-making significance in the history of China's poetry development.

Second, Su Shi pushed ci poetry of the Song Dynasty to an unprecedented brand new height and state in terms of contents, forms, skills and styles. On the one hand, Su Shi fully expanded ci poems'

Picture of Writing a Poem on Bamboos, painted by Du Jin in the Ming Dynasty. The person writing a poem on bamboos with a writing brush is Su Dongpo. Dongpo loved bamboos, and once said, "I'd rather eat no meat than live without bamboos."

73

contents to include patriotic feelings, life philosophy, historical stories, concrete objects, travels, Buddhist doctrines, visits to mountains, departure, mediation on the past, mourning for the dead, rural sentiments and pastoral scenery, and greatly broadened the scope of life and art for ci poetry creation. Liu Xizai, a literary critic of the Qing Dynasty, called Dongpo's ci poems "can express all things and describe all things." Apart from expansion of contents, Su's ci poetry also reached a deeply moving state in terms of expression of emotions. *Riverside Town* written by him to mourn for his deceased wife is an example:

Ten boundless years now separate the living and the dead,
I have not often thought of her, but neither can I forget.
Her lonely grave is a thousand li distant, I can't say where my wife lies cold.
We could not recognize each other even if we met again,
My face is all but covered with dust, my temples glazed with frost.
In deepest night, a sudden dream returns me to my homeland,
She sits before a little window, and sorts her dress and make-up.
We look at each other without a word, a thousand tears now flow.
I must accept that every year I'll think of that heart breaking place,
Where the moon shines brightly in the night, and bare pines guard the tomb.

Here, there are both tender feelings between the husband and wife and boundless melancholy about life; both lonely and sad feelings revealed after the wife's death and his courage to face the miserable and bleak life. This short ci poem contains graceful, unaffected and moving expressions full of twists and turns with lingering charm.

Third, Su's ci poems formed an independent style, and under its influence and push, the school of spectacular bold and unrestrained ci poetry was formed. Before Su Shi, the "graceful and restrained" style of ci poetry was dominant. Su's ci poems changed this situation, brought a powerful new trend to the circles of ci poets, diversified ci poetry creation methods other than those of creating graceful and restrained poems, and strengthened ci poetry creation. Su's ci poems are bold and unrestrained in all aspects. Historical stories, descriptions of people, depictions of concrete objects, images, momentum and scenes in Su's ci poems all reflect the intensity of emotions, the rhythm of words and the profoundness of meanings. The boldness, unrestraint and solemnity of Su's ci poems are moving. *Charm of a Maiden Singer – Memories of the Past at Red Cliff* is a classic representative of the bold and unrestrained style of Su's ci poetry:

The endless river eastward flows;
With its huge waves are gone all those
Gallant heroes of bygone years.
West of the ancient fortress appears
Red Cliff where General Zhou won his early fame
When the Three Kingdom were in flame.
Rocks tower in the air and waves teat on the shore,
Rolling up a thousand heaps of snow.
To match the land so fair, how many heroes of yore

Picture of the Red Cliff, painted by Wu Yuanzhi in the Jin Dynasty, shows the scene of Su Shi and his friend drifting about on a boat at the Red Cliff.

Had made great show!
I fancy General Zhou at the height
Of his success, with a plume fan in hand,
In a silk hood, so brave and bright,
Laughing and jesting with his bride so fair,
While enemy ships were destroyed as planned
Like castles in the air.
Should their souls revisit this land,
Sentimental, his bride would laugh to say;
Younger than they, I have my hair turned grey.
Life is but like a dream.
On moon, I drink to you who have seen them on the stream.

"The endless river eastward flows" is a beginning with great momentum, bringing readers to the sky of the glorious, magnificent and stormy history. Su Dongpo with the deep emotions and sharp eyes of a politician commented on national affairs and appraised people. Time, space and language all changed with the poet's flow of thought. There are lines with great momentum such as "Rocks tower in the air and waves teat on the shore, rolling up a thousand heaps of snow" and murmurs such as "I fancy General Zhou at the height of his success, with a plume fan in hand, in a silk hood, so brave and bright, laughing and jesting with his bride so fair." They are powerful and unstrained like a heavenly steed soaring across the skies, not limited to one type, reflecting the charm of Su's bold and unrestrained ci poems in a classic manner.

Su's bold, unrestrained, unconventional and original ci poems opened new space for development of ci poetry of the Song Dynasty, and made special contributions to further establishing ci poetry's status in the history of literature. Under the influence of Su's ci poems, the bold and unrestrained school of ci poetry was formed in the Song Dynasty. Huang Tingjian (1045–1105), Chao Buzhi (1053–1110), etc. carried forward the style of Su's ci poetry in the Northern Song Dynasty, and Xin Qiji (1140–1207) in the Southern Song Dynasty developed the bold and unrestrained style of Su's ci poems and brought about a more magnificent situation. It needs to be pointed out that the outstanding achievements and huge influence of Su Shi's bold and unrestrained

Picture of the poetic sentiment of ci-poem *Prelude to Water Melody*, painted by contemporary Liu Dawei

ci poems do not mean his denial of the graceful and restrained school's ci poems. Su Shi himself also wrote many graceful and restrained works. This just shows that to establish a new style, it is most important to break with the original pattern boldly and be good at pioneer new trends.

Li Qingzhao and Graceful and Restrained Ci Poetry

Li Qingzhao (1084–1155), with the courtesy name of Yian Jushi, was a famous female ci poet living between the late Northern Song Dynasty and the early Southern Song Dynasty, and a very influential female writer in the history of Chinese literature. Li Qingzhao was born in a scholar-bureaucrat's family, well educated in literature in her childhood, and accomplished in literature and history with outstanding talent. She and her husband Zhao Mingcheng were both interested in collecting and studying epigraphic calligraphy and painting works, and wrote *Epigraphic Collection*.

Li Qingzhao's life includes two periods separated by the Jingkang Incident. In the 2nd year of the Jingkang Period (1127), Jin troops captured the capital of the Northern Song Dynasty Dongjing (today's Kaifeng, Henan), and the Song Dynasty moved the capital to Lin'an (today's Hangzhou, Zhejiang) in the

Figure of Li Qingzhao, painted by Cui Cuo in the Qing Dynasty

south and was historically called the Southern Song Dynasty. Before the capital was moved to the south, Li Qingzhao lived happily as a girl and young married woman. She had her joy and happiness. Though her husband served as an official away from home, adding some loneliness and grief of parting, her life was quiet and comfortable. After the capital was moved to the south, the country was conquered and her family wrecked. She wandered from place to place among fires of war. Besides, her husband died of illness, and the epigraphic calligraphy and painting works collected in many years were lost. All miseries in life attacked at the same time, making Li Qingzhao sink into a sad and painful situation. The Jingkang Incident completely changed Li Qingzhao's life and changed her understanding of literature. Before the incident, she was a daughter of an eminent family, she and her husband loved each other, and her family life was the main part of her life; after the incident, the country was conquered and her family wrecked, she wandered from place to place, and the fate of the country became an issue she had to think about. This also added deep awareness of potential dangers and melancholy to her later literary creations.

In *On Ci Poetry*, Li Qingzhao systematically elaborated her views on creation of ci poetry and schools of ci poetry. Like Su Shi and others, she emphasized the difference between poetry and ci poetry and that ci poetry should "be a separate genre" different from poetry. However, Li Qingzhao more clearly pointed out ci poetry's fundamental characteristics should be elegance, simplicity, smoothness, flexibility, strict sound and rhyme patterns, solemnity and exquisiteness. Li Qingzhao not only separated ci poetry and poetry, but also pointed out the characteristics of the graceful and restrained style of ci poetry commended by her.

Li Qingzhao's ci poems reveal his stylistic characteristics of softness, mildness and exquisiteness. This is first of all related to her sharp perceptiveness particular to women. Li Qingzhao's ci poems have a very prominent image, i.e. the lyric protagonist's sentimental, emotional and sorrowful image. Through this image, the female ci poet repeatedly expressed her deep consciousness and feelings from the bottom of her heart tenderly and insightfully. Her famous ci poem *Like A Dream* is an example:

Last night the wind was strong and rain was fine,
Sound sleep did not dispel the taste of wine.
I ask the maid who's rolling up the screen.

"The same crab-apple tree," she says, "is seen."
"Don't you know,
Don't you know
The red should languish and the green must grow?"

This ci poem has not only the artistic conceptions of "night rain" and "fragrant flowers" often described in previous ci poems, but also its own unique characteristics. This short ci poem features skillful and changeful methods such as word reduplication and Q&A. The length of one's life and "growing green and languish red" form a sharp contrast and make people feel boundless melancholy. *A Twig of Mume Blossoms* is more delicate and grieved:

The jade-like mat feels autumn's cold, I change a coat
And 'mid the fading fragrance
Of lotus pink alone I boat.
Will wild returning geese bring letters through the cloud?
When they come, with moonbeams
My west chamber's overflowed.
As water flows and flowers fall without leaving traces,
One and the same longing
Overflows two lonely places.
I cannot get rid of this sorrow: kept apart
From my eyebrows,
It gnaws my heart.

This ci poem was written after the newly-married couple of Li Qingzhao and Zhao Mingcheng parted. Though expressing personal feelings, it is vivid and moving. The character's expressions and movements as well as the slightest emotional stirrings from the bottom of the heart are described in great detail. What should be commended is that Li Qingzhao used plain words to express such an exceedingly sentimental and complicated emotion without difficulty. "From my eyebrows, it gnaws my heart" perfectly manifests the lovesickness that could not be dispelled by the woman separated from her husband.

Her famous work *Intoxicated Under the Shadow of Flowers* is also a ci poem on her longing for her husband:

The Double Ninth Festival
Light mists and heavy clouds,
melancholy the long dreary day.
In the golden censer
the burning incense is dying away.
It is again time
for the lovely Double-Ninth Festival;
The coolness of midnight
penetrates my screen of sheer silk
and chills my pillow of jade.
After drinking wine at twilight
under the chrysanthemum hedge,
My sleeves are perfumed
by the fragrance of the plants.
Oh, I cannot say it is not endearing,
Only, when the west wind stirs the curtain,
I see that I am more gracile
than the yellow flowers.

There is also a story about this ci poem. During the Double Ninth Festival, Li Qingzhao wrote this ci poem and mailed it to her husband. After Zhao Mingcheng read it, he appreciated it very much but wanted to surpass his wife, so he closed the door to visitors, cudgeled his brains for three days and three nights, wrote 50 ci poems, mixed the ci poem written by his wife with them, and showed them to a friend. After perusing them, the friend thought for a while and finally said that "Oh, I cannot say it is not endearing, only, when the west wind stirs the curtain, I see that I am more

gracile than the yellow flowers" were the best lines!

Li Qingzhao was also very good at expressing complicated emotions with ci poems' rhymes and embodying those indescribable inner feelings in common actual scenes. *Slow, Slow Tune* is a representative ci poem among Li Qingzhao's later works:

I look for what I miss,
I know not what it is:
I feel so sad, so drear,
So lonely, without cheer.
How hard is it
To keep me fit
In this lingering cold!
Hardly warmed up
By cup on cup
Of wine so dry.
Oh! how could I
Endure at dusk the drift
Of wind so swift?
It breaks my heart, alas!
To see the wild geese pass,
For they are my acquaintances of old.
The ground is covered with yellow flowers
Faded and fallen in showers.
Who will pick them up now?
Sitting alone at the window,
How could I but quicken
The pace of darkness which won't thicken?
On parasol-trees a fine rain drizzles
As twilight grizzles.

Picture of a Beauty Beside Parasol-trees, painted by Wang Su in the Qing Dynasty. This picture depicts the poetic sentiment of Li Qingzhao's ci-poem *Intoxicated Under the Shadow of Flowers* by contrasting the real person and unreal scenery and setting off the artistic conception, "Only, when the west wind stirs the curtain, I see that I am more gracile than the yellow flowers."

Picture of the poetic sentiment of ci-poem *The Butterfly Loves Flowers*, painted by contemporary Xiao Huizhu. To express her longing for her husband and her solitude of living alone, Li Qingzhao wrote in the ci-poem, "Will anyone drink wine, or compose poems with me? Tears streak my powered face, and my hairpins are too heavy to wear."

Oh! What can I do with a grief
Beyond belief!

The cold and lifeless natural scene of late autumn is also a portrayal of sadness in life. Here Li Qingzhao spared no effort to describe the scene of late autumn, and the ci poet showed her inner emotions in writing at the same time. Her resentment about the conquered country and wrecked family, her misery of homelessness and the loneliness she felt after her husband's death were all released. However, the ci poem is common and clear without flowery language. "My acquaintances of old," "who will pick them up now" and "what can I do with a grief beyond belief" are all very plain lines. Alliteration and assonance in the first few lines are also very common, but this is just where Li Qingzhao's skills lie. Profound meanings are embodied in common words, and plain expressions are filled with a sense of beauty. Those seemingly common words are easy-to-read and highly musical.

In both the early period and the late period, Li Qingzhao established her unique position in the history of literature with the graceful and restrained style. Her ci poems were reputed by later people as "Yi'an style" and "orthodox graceful and restrained style."

Xin Qiji and Bold and Unconstrained Ci Poetry

Figure of Xin Qiji

After Su Dongpo pioneered bold and unrestrained ci poetry, the styles of ci poetry of the Song Dynasty began to change, and the graceful and restrained style and the bold and unrestrained style both shone, pushing the bold and unrestrained style of ci poetry of the Song Dynasty to a new climax.

Xin Qiji, with the courtesy name of Youan and the alias of Jiaxuan, was a patriotic person of ideals and integrity and a great ci poet. He wrote *Jiaxuan's Ci Poetry*. Politically, Xin Qiji was a representative figure of hawks, resolutely advocating the northern expedition for recovering the land of the Song Dynasty. He showed "in his lifetime, he had the extraordinary powers and took pride in his integrity and achievements." This righteous, just and patriotic political attitude exerted important influence on Xin Qiji's ci poetry.

In terms of literature, Xin Qiji emphasized that current events, social changes, thoughts and feelings should be important contents and basic tenets of literary creation. In particular, a person's lofty spirit should be a source of literary works' charm. He did not agree to the view that literary works should only manifest "vicissitudes of life" and "love and resentment:" "Weal and woe, old and new, joy to meet, grief to part, all come in view. Not only waves will rise by riverside, the way of the world is hard far and wide." (*Partridges in the Sky*) He particularly expressed his discontent with the excessive emphasis on the organization of ci poetry of the Song Dynasty and the excessive pursuit of exquisite modes of expression: "I intend to write works as magnificent as the Taishan Mountain and Huangshan Mountain instead of skillful and exquisite works" (*Immortal at the River*). He attached importance to emotion and momentum, and did his best to advocate the extremely powerful, bold and unrestrained style of ci poetry: "The poetry world is quite lofty, pens are like mountains, and ink is like streams" (*Spring in a Pleasure Garden*).

Xin's ci poems contain abundant and profound thoughts and emotions as well as his unique personal life experience, showing distinctive individual traits. Among Xin's ci poems, his patriotic ci poems are most emotional and widely influential. Different from ordinary writers and poets, Xin Qiji was first of all a warrior experienced in battle. His army life of charging, fighting and hardship made his patriotic feelings vivid and weighty. Expression of battlefield experiences and feelings became the most prominent characteristic of Xin's ci

Picture of the poetic sentiment of ci-poem *Joy of Eternal Union – Recalling the Past at the Beigu Pavilion of Jingkou*, painted by contemporary Wang Guoxin

poetry. *Dance of the Cavalry – Words of Encouragement* sent to Chen Tongfu is a representative of such works:

Though drunk, we lit the lamp to see the glaive;
Sober, we heard the horns from tent to tent.
Under the flags, beef grilled
Was eaten by our warriors brave
And martial airs were played by fifty instruments:
'T was an autumn maneuver in the field.
On gallant steed,
Running full speed,
We'd shoot with twanging bows
Recovering the lost land for the sovereign,
'This everlasting fame that we would win.
But alas! White hair grows!

The thrilling scenes of lighting the lamp to see the glaive, returning to the army in a dream and reviewing soldiers in autumn can only be appreciated and understood by those with personal experience. However, "But alas! White hair grows!" expresses another feeling of Xin Qiji, i.e. the small imperial court of the Southern Song Dynasty content to retain sovereignty over a part of the country did not have the will to fight against the enemy but surrendered wholeheartedly and sought temporary peace. This made all patriotic persons of ideals and integrity including Xin Qiji unable to dedicate themselves to the service of their country. They felt sad because their enthusiasm and lofty ideals were in vain. This emotion runs deeply in many ci poems by Xin Qiji. *Bodhisattva-like Barbarians – Written on the wall of Zaokou in Jiangxi Province* is one of them:

The clear river water below Yugu Terrace;
How many tears in it – tears of the travelers.
If want to see Chang'an in the northwest,

It's pitiful beyond many a hillcrest.
The verdant mountains cannot block its flow;
After all towards the east it does go.
At dusk on the river I am grieving,
Hearing in deep mountains partridges tweeting.

In his late years, Xin Qiji defended Jingkou (i.e. Zhenjiang, Jiangsu). On the one hand, he still waited expectantly for the northern expedition, but on the other hand, he saw the cowardice of the rulers of the Southern Song Dynasty more clearly. Though Xin Qiji was in extremely painful conflict, he still deeply cherished faith in recovering the north and regaining the homeland. His work *Joy of Eternal Union – Recalling the Past at the Beigu Pavilion of Jingkou* expresses deep and complicated emotions in a bleak and gloomy style but is still unrestrained, powerful and full of heroic spirit. It is an important representative work of Xi's ci poems:

The land is boundless as of yore,
But nowhere can be found
A hero like the king defending southern shore.
The singing hall, the dancing ground,
All gallant deeds now sent away
By driving wind and blinding rain!
The slanting sun sheds its departing ray
O'er tree-shaded and grassy lane
Where lived the Cowherd King retaking the lost land.
In bygone years,
Leading armed cavaliers,
With golden spear in hand,
Tigerlike, he had slain
The foe on the thousand-mile Central Plain.
His son launched in haste a northern campaign;
Defeated at Mount Wolf, he shed his tears in vain.

Picture of the poetic sentiment of ci-poem
Green Jade Table – Lantern Festival,
painted by contemporary Feng Da

I still remember three and forty years ago
The thriving town destroyed in flames by the foe.
How can I bear
To see the chief aggressor's shrine
Worshipped 'mid crows and drumbeats as divine?
Who would still care
If an old general
Is strong enough to take back the lost capital?
Where is the Central Plain?

Xin's ci poems are grand, vivid with distinctive images, ambitious, highly emotional and unrestrained, integrating description of people and events, blending feelings and settings naturally, themed on the past and present and not limited to one type. Xin Qiji's greater contribution was that he developed and promoted the bold and unrestrained style of ci poetry pioneered by Su Shi, pushed the bold, unrestrained and powerful style of ci poetry of the Song Dynasty to the extreme, and made it a general trend. From Su Shi to Xin Qiji, the bold and unrestrained school of ci poetry of the Song Dynasty was officially formed. Wang Shizhen (1634—1711) who lived in the Qing Dynasty made the following comment on Xin's ci poems: "They are fervent, free, and extremely arrogant. He changed the tunes of famous ci poets, suddenly came to the fore, and formed a unique style other than the exquisite feminine style, which still exists today."

Xin Qiji's ci poems like those of Su Dongpo are mostly bold, unrestrained and powerful works and graceful, restrained and beautiful works. *Green Jade Table – Lantern Festival* is obscure, restrained, charming, moving and meaningful:

One night's east wind adorns a thousand trees with flowers
And blows down stars in showers.
Fine steeds and carved cabs spread fragrance en route;
Music vibrates from the flute;
The moon sheds its full light
While fish and dragon lanterns dance all night.
In gold-thread dress, with moth or willow ornaments,
Giggling, she melts into the throng with trails of scents
But in the crowd once and again
I look for her in vain.
When all at once I turn my head,
I find her there where lantern light is dimly shed.

Great poets and great ci poets from Su Shi to Xin Qiji were all versatile instead of limiting themselves to one type.

Late Maturity of Drama

The form of Chinese ancient drama is traditional Chinese opera integrating literature, music, dances and performances. Traditional Chinese opera, ancient Greek drama and Indian Sanskrit drama are collectively called "the world's three ancient drama types." Compared with ancient Greek drama and Indian Sanskrit drama, traditional Chinese opera matured late and took shape in the Song and Yuan dynasties (the 12th and 13th century). Though it was born late, traditional Chinese drama's vitality was stronger. Chinese drama maintained its basic form in more than 800 years and is still welcomed by many people.

In the long course of development, several important forms of Chinese classical drama emerged, including southern drama of the Song and Yuan dynasties, poetic drama of the Yuan Dynasty and legends of the Ming and Qing Dynasties.

Great Yuan Drama Writer Guan Hanqing

Guan Hanqing (c. 1220–1300), a native of Dadu (today's Beijing), was called one of the "four masters of Yuan drama." He was a playwright with a strong personality, unique style and abundant experience in artistic practice and the first great playwright well known both at home and abroad in the history of Chinese drama. He created more than 60 poetic dramas in his lifetime, and exerted important and far-reaching influence on the development of Chinese drama. Guan Hanqing's pursuits of perfect drama and perfect righteous character were integrated. *In Do Not Give in to Old Age*, he gave vent to his mental character and dramatic character:

Figure of Guan Hanqing, painted by contemporary Li Hu

I am a copper pea that can withstand steaming, boiling, hammering and stir-frying... I will never stop no matter what misfortunes befall me, whether my teeth fall out, my mouth turns crooked, my legs are crippled, or my arms broken.

"A cooper pea" is the truest and most vivid portrayal of Guan Hanqing's image and his life attitude of resisting and fighting bravely, never giving in to restrictions of feudal traditions, never yielding to mundane pressure and never readily subscribing to hypocrites' views. This spiritual quality ran through all dramas created by Guan Hanqing and his lifelong practice of character.

Guan Hanqing's achievements in drama creation are mainly manifested in poetic drama of the Yuan Dynasty, which is a kind of traditional Chinese opera sung to northern tunes. The so-called northern tunes are tunes formed on the basis of traditional music such as greater tunes and various modes of ancient Chinese music through absorption of northern folk tunes and minority ethnic groups' songs, different from the tunes popular in the south. Poetic drama has its unique style. The basic form is four acts in one play. Each act is a section of a story, sometimes added with a prologue to adjust plot changes. Poetic drama's librettos are written according to certain modes of ancient Chinese music and tunes. Each of the four acts in one play uses a mode of ancient Chinese music and only one rhyme pattern.

Guan Hanqing's dramas not only truly reflect various aspects of social life in that period, shaping many different types of stage images, but also manifest deep thoughts and clear love and hate, including angry accusations of power and influence, biting satires on common customs, real sympathy with the

A mural painting in Guangsheng Temple, Hongdong County, Shanxi demonstrates the scene of a performance of poetic drama of the Yuan Dynasty.

Illustration in *The Injustice to Dou E that Touched Heaven and Earth*

oppressed and humiliated and heartfelt praises for the indomitable. His dramas are classified into three main categories: works accusing and attacking the dark side of social reality represented by *The Injustice to Dou E*; works warmly praising witty and brave women represented by *The Riverside Pavilion* and *Saving the Dusty-windy*; works eulogizing historical heroic figures to convey real feelings with history represented by *Meeting the Enemies Alone*.

Among Guan Hanqing's numerous poetic dramas, the most influential work most representative of his ideological state and artistic level is *The Injustice to Dou E*. This drama on the one hand reflects the theme of profound Chinese literary traditions and depicts resolute fight against the feudal system oppressing and devastating humanity, and on the other hand ruthlessly exposes the darkness and injustice in real social life in the Yuan Dynasty and criticizes the thoughts, morals and life customs maintaining the feudal system at a deeper level.

Stage photo of the meeting of Dou E's ghost and her father in *The Injustice to Dou E*

The plot of *The Injustice to Dou E* is mainly the story of Dou E, a young girl suffering an uncorrected wrong and fighting till death. Dou E's father is exploited by usurious loan lenders and has to sell his seven-year-old daughter to Granny Cai as a child bride. When Dou E is 20 years old, Zhang Lü'er takes a liking to her. To force Dou E to marry him, Zhang Lü'er kills his own father by mistake with the original intention of poisoning Granny Cai to death, but he falsely accuses Dou E as the killer. As a result, Dou E confesses to the false charge under torture and dies tragically on the execution ground. The plot of *The Injustice to Dou E* is not complex, but there are many shocking scenes. Dou E has three highlights. First, she resolutely resists the rude and overbearing acts of Zhang Lü'er and his father and resolutely opposes her mother-in-law's life attitude of dragging out an ignoble existence; second, Dou E confesses to the false charge under torture not because she cannot withstand torture but because she cannot bear to see her mother-in-law being tortured cruelly; third, before Dou E is executed, she makes "three vows," sticking to her innocence, fighting till her death and manifesting the ordinary woman's fearless heroic spirit. Through Dou E's tragic fate, Guan Hanqing attacked the corrupt system and the dark side of the society in that period, and at the same time warmly eulogized the righteousness shown by Dou E and her spirit of fighting till the end despite the weakness of individuals. As Dou E sings in [Rolling Ball] aria:

The sun and moon give light by day and by night,
Mountains and rivers watch over the world of men;
Yet Heaven cannot tell the innocent from the guilty;
And confuses the wicked with the good!
The good are poor, and die before their time;
The wicked are rich, and live to a great old age.
The gods are afraid of the mighty and bully the weak;
They let evil take its course.
Ah, Earth! you will not distinguish good from bad,
And, Heaven! you let me suffer this injustice!
Tears pour down my cheeks in vain!

The Injustice to Dou E from the prologue to the four acts in the play combines a high degree of reality and strong emotion. Particularly, Dou E makes "three vows" before her death. First, if injustice has indeed been done, when the sword strikes off my head, not a drop of my warm blood will stain the ground. It will all fly up instead to the white silk streamer twelve feet long. Second, this is the hottest time of summer. If injustice has indeed been done, three feet of snow will cover my dead body. Third, Chuzhou will suffer from drought for three whole years. The "three vows" of Dou E all come true. These plots full of romantic imagination greatly enhance the drama's tragic atmosphere. It can really be called "The Injustice to Dou E that Touched Heaven and Earth!"

Modern scholar Wang Guowei (1877–1927) highly commended the tragic significance of *The Injustice to Dou E* in *The History of Drama of the Song and Yuan Dynasties*, "The most tragic dramas such as *The Injustice to Dou E* by Guan Hanqing and *The Orphan of Zhao* by Ji Junxiang deserve to be ranked among the world's great tragic dramas because though the protagonists are framed by evil people, they still risk their own lives out of their will."

Romance of the West Chamber, a Never-failing Drama

It is said that *Romance of the West Chamber*, also called *Cui Yingying Waiting in the West Chamber in a Full-moon Night*, was written by Yuan playwright Wang Shifu (the years of his birth and death are unknown). In more than 700 years, it prospered through time on the stage of drama, exerted far-reaching influence on the creation of dramas on the theme of love in later ages, and became a classic drama widely known in China.

Romance of the West Chamber is based on *Yingying's Biography*, a legend novel written by Yuan Zhen (779–831) in the Tang Dynasty. With the theme of "wishing all lovers in the world could be united in marriage," it demonstrates the thought of opposing feudal ethical codes and pursuing marital autonomy, which was of major progressive significance back then. "The daughter of the prime minister" Cui Yingying and "the son of a high official" Zhang Sheng, under the help of the Red Maid, break from the bondage of feudal ethical

Statue of Cui Yingying, painted by Qiu Ying in the Ming Dynasty. Yingying burning joss sticks and praying to the moon in the picture is a scene in the poetic drama.

codes, overcome the obstruction of people around them, eliminate their mutual misunderstanding and finally unite in marriage as two people loving each other after twists and turns. They encounter a lot of difficulties in the pursuit of marital autonomy, but comic plots are often added for characters in pain in the work, making their images more concrete and vivid.

The above contents include complicated dramatic conflicts mainly along two lines. One is the conflict between Cui Yingying's mother the old lady, etc. and Cui Yingying, Zhang Sheng, the Red Maid, etc., which is the conflict between young people pursuing marital autonomy and conservative feudal forces; the second is the conflict among Cui Yingying, Zhang Sheng and the Red Maid, which is mainly misunderstanding. The former line of conflict as the "primary line" and the latter line of conflict as the "secondary line" complement each other and are mingled, making the plot of

Illustration in *Romance of the West Chamber*. Yingying is reading a letter from her lover, and the Red Maid is prying behind a screen.

Romance of the West Chamber full of soul-stirring twists and turns and making the dramatic effect more intense and vivid.

Most characters in *Romance of the West Chamber* have complex thoughts and personalities. While depicting characters, the author abandoned the restrictive stereotypes, categories and models in ancient drama. Zhang Sheng admires Yingying's beauty and talent and passionately courts Yingying, but he does not seem frivolous in this course because he is an aristocratic family's well-educated son after all. Cui Yingying bravely pursues freedom of love and marital autonomy, but because of the feudal education received by her, she still has many obstacles in her mind.

The Red Maid is a glorious image in *Romance of the West Chamber*. Though she is just Yingying's servant girl, her arias account for one third of the whole drama, showing her position in this drama. The resourceful, chivalrous and fearless Red Maid acts as a go-between for Yingying and Zhang Sheng, helps them eliminate misunderstanding, gives counsel to them, and assists them to deal with the old lady's interference and obstruction. She can be called their counsellor. Tang Xianzu highly commended the Red Maid, "She has both talent and braveness. With her as the counsellor, what problems can't be solved?"

The old lady is a representative of feudal parents. Though she is a lesser role in the drama, this image is quite brilliant. She exists as the opponent to Yingying and Zhang Sheng's pursuit of marital autonomy. On the other hand, she loves her daughter Yingying, handles affairs prudently, manages the household properly, and shoulders the family's heavy burden after her husband's death. On the other hand, she sticks to feudal ethical codes, asks Yingying to marry Zheng Heng according to her father's will, and hopes to revive the family through marriage. However, when she finds that Yingying and Zhang Sheng are determined to be together, she figures out the half measure of imperial examinations. Therefore, the old lady's image is not obstinate either but constantly enriched with the changes in situations and thoughts.

Linguistically, *Romance of the West Chamber* contains flowery language and many classic lines popular all the time. Qing novelist Cao Xueqin highly praised *Romance of the West Chamber* in *Dream of the Red Chamber* through the heroine Lin Daiyu: "It contains admonitory lines with a lingering flavor."

Wang Shifu was quite good at depicting characters' inner feelings exquisitely in depth,

capturing their inner pleasure, anger, sorrow and joy, thus touching readers' hearts, writing emotionally and moving people with emotion. The aria [Farewell at the Pavilion] is an example:

With clouds the sky turns grey
O'er yellow-bloom-paved way.
How bitter blows the western breeze!
From north to south fly the wild geese.
Why like wine-flushed face is frosted forest red?
It's dyed in tears the parting lovers shed.
It's my regret
So late we met;
It grieves my heart
So soon to part.
Long as the willow branch may be,
It cannot tie his parting steed to the tree.
What would I not have done
If autumn forest could hang up the setting sun!
Go slowly, parting steed;
Cab, follow it with speed!
Of lovesickness just cured,
The grief of parting must now be endured.
"I'm going," when a voice is heard to say.
My body seems to waste away.
When the Pavilion of Farewell comes in sight,
My bracelet becomes no longer tight.
Who knows, who knows
My heart full of woes?

This area depicts the scene of Zhang Sheng's departure from Yingying at the Pavilion of Farewell for imperial examinations in the capital. It sets off the protagonists' feelings with colorful natural scenery and depicts Yingying's sadness, anxiety, worry and longing at this moment, blending feelings and settings and moving people deeply.

The theme of *Romance of the West Chamber*, i.e. "wishing all lovers in the world could be united in marriage," has moved innumerable people. Therefore, *Romance of the West Chamber* is a never-failing drama reputed as "the best work among all new poetic dramas and old legends."

Tang Xianzu's Drama Legends

In the Ming and Qing dynasties, the development of Chinese ancient drama entered a new stage – the times of legends. Compared with poetic drama of the Yuan Dynasty, legends have longer scripts and more complex plots. Works of various types such as historical dramas, dramas on customs, dramas on current affairs and social dramas emerged as the times required. Meanwhile, dramatic roles in legends underwent great development and eliminated the restriction of one leading actor in poetic drama of the Yuan Dynasty.

Most legend writers of the Ming and Qing dynasties were scholars, and the most important representative figure among them was Tang Xianzu (1550–1616). Tang Xianzu, a native of Linchuan, Jiangxi, passed the imperial examinations at the provincial level, served as an official, and had great literary fame and innate pride. Later he was demoted because he submitted a written statement to the imperial court to criticize current malpractices. These experiences deepened Tang Xianzu's understanding of the society and rulers. In the 26th year of the Wanli Period (1598), he thoroughly resigned from his official post to focus on creation of dramas. He completed his most famous representative

Figure of Tang Xianzu

drama *The Peony Pavilion* in this year, and later completed *Record of Southern Bough* and *Record of Handan* to finish his "Four Dreams of Linchuan," the other one being *The Purple Hairpin* he wrote earlier.

Tang Xianzu advocated nature, paid attention to dispositions, and held the view that "feelings" should be "natural." In the final analysis, his creation of dramas was just for "feelings!" In Tang Xianzu's masterpiece The Peony Pavilion, "feelings" are manifested vividly.

The plot of *The Peony Pavilion* is mainly based on the vernacular novel *The Revival of Du Liliang for Love*. In this novel, the daughter of the Prefect of Nanxiong dies from her preoccupation with a dream after walking in a garden during the reign of Emperor Guangzong of the Song Dynasty. Before her death, she paints a miniature, which is obtained by Liu Mengmei, the son of Prefect Liu. Liu Mengmei thinks about her day and night, and thus meets Liniang's ghost. At last, her grave is opened to revive her, and Du and Liu get married. This is a story mingled with reality, dreams, truth and absurdity. Such themes were not rare in the history of Chinese ancient literature, but why is Tang Xianzu's *The Peony Pavilion* so moving? This is related to Tang Xianzu's pursuit of "feelings." In his work, young men and women's experience and pursuit of true love are so justified and urgent! Apart from Tang Xianzu's style of writing, the reason why *The Peony Pavilion* can touch people's hearts deeply is that it has a special historical and social background. In thousands of years, the feudal system and ideological oppression devastated innumerable people's normal emotion, lust, yearning for and pursuit of beautiful love. Du Liniang who persistently pursues beautiful love as if intoxicated and stupefied regardless of her life has touched the hearts of innumerable young men and women. "Where is the pleasant day and pretty sight? Who can enjoy contentment and delight?" These popular lines in *The Peony Pavilion* integrate human nature and beautiful natural scenery and show yearning for freedom and defense for human rights most truthfully and directly. Therefore, *The Peony Pavilion* demonstrates persistent pursuit for nature and human relations rather than profound ideological connotations!

Du Liniang is the core image in *The Peony Pavilion*. Her image is glorious because she is innocent and pure with abundant inner feelings and refined emotions. Du Liniang is knowledgeable, reasonable and conventional, but her oppressed and restricted nature, once released, forms an unstoppable emotional impulse and a bold force for pursuit of beautiful love. In the scene of *A Walk in the Garden*, Du Liniang, "summoned from dream by orioles' trill," embraces spring for the first time in her life, and the girl's pure desire for love is aroused by infinite attractive beauty of nature. Thus, her yearning for beautiful love in the world is further stimulated. Tang Xianzu meticulously depicted Du Liniang's psychological activities in this course and expressed her extremely complicated inner changes. She marvels at the beauty of spring and the beauty of the freedom of flowers and birds; she sighs for transient spring and youth; she feels endless sadness for her oppression. These depictions form the basis of Du Liniang's "interrupted dream" and urge her to realize her wishes in dreams. Du Liniang's image not only symbolizes fight against ethical codes and pursuit of freedom of love, but also contains the cultural connotation of humanity's return to nature. The fundamental charm of this image lies in elimination of the boundary between feelings and reasons and, more importantly, expression of irresistible nature and humanity! This is the reason why *The Peony Pavilion* can transcend space and time and still have strong artistic appeal today.

Sought Dream, *Interrupted Dream*, an illustration in *The Peony Pavilion*

The dramatic structure of *The Peony Pavilion* combines realism and imagination from reality to dreams and from the world to the afterworld, but it is reasonable and flexible. "A walk in the garden and the interrupted dream" is the most important section of *The Peony Pavilion*. "The walk in the garden" arouses Du Liniang's love, which is irreversible but can hardly be realized in reality. Therefore, she has to pursue and realize it in dreams. This naturally leads to the scene of Du Liniang and her lover Liu Mengmei meeting and getting acquainted with each other at the Peony Pavilion. "The interrupted dream" is great because it is both "interrupted" and "uninterrupted," and the interruption is unreasonable but makes sense. As Tang Xianzu said himself, "Dreams are formed by feelings, and the drama is formed by dreams."

The Peony Pavilion also represents great linguistic and artistic achievements. The most prominent one among them is individualized language. Different characters and different scenes in the drama are depicted with different language including literary language reflecting scholars' accomplishments and daily language from various social strata. Diversified language makes *The Peony Pavilion*, whether read as a drama script or performed on the stage, lively and magnificent, always maintaining strong artistic appeal. The following section of *The Interrupted Dream* is an example:

[Around the Pond]
(Main female character enters) Summoned from dream, by orioles' trill.
Sparkling light of the new year,
Fills this "cloistered courtyard," where I stand.
(Supporting female character) Douse the heavy incense,
Toss – the silk floss ends.
Will this spring time be the same as last year?
(Crows Crying at Night) "(Main female character) Dawn hides the Plum Blossom Ridge.
My hair tangled by sleep.
(Supporting female character) Your spring chignon aslant, leaning against the balustrade.
(Main female character) Can scissors cut, or comb untangle?
This endless weariness.
(Supporting female character) I've bid flowers and birds to speed up springtime."

Small Portrait of Du Liniang, painted by Pan Gongshou in the Qing Dynasty

(Main female character) Spring Fragrance,
Have you told the gardener to sweep the garden path?
(Supporting female character) I have done so.
(Main female character) Bring the mirror over here.
(Supporting female character enters with the mirror stand and clothes) "She faces the mirror when done with her coiffure;
She adds perfume before donning her silken gown."
The mirror stand and clothes are here.

These simple and diversified lines including sung, spoken parts and scene descriptions are complicated but not confusing with clear layers, fully reflecting Tang Xianzu's superb ability to master language. Different from the Yuan poetic drama's expression form of four acts in one play using the same rhyme pattern, Ming legends are mostly serialized with sung and spoken parts for various roles featuring more diversified expression methods and linguistic modes. *The Peony Pavilion* is a good example.

The Peony Pavilion with magical artistic thoughts and sublime human glory has

Stage photo of the Kunqu drama *The Peony Pavilion*

become an enduring work in the history of Chinese drama. There are many later versions of *The Peony Pavilion* and many annotated versions. Contemporary Bai Xianyong and others changed the Kunqu drama *The Peony Pavilion* into the "Youth Version," which is liked by young people around the world. This proves the great charm of *The Peony Pavilion* and Chinese ancient dramas again.

Peak of Novels

The concept of "small tales" emerged first in *Zhuangzi – What comes from Without*: "Those who dress up their small tales to obtain favor with the magistrates are far from being men of great understanding." Here "small tales" mainly refers to trivial hearsay. "Novels" as a literary genre emerged first in the Tang Dynasty and were called "legends" then. Generally speaking, Chinese ancient novels underwent three courses of great development: first, people of the Tang Dynasty "began to write novels" including representative legends of the Tang Dynasty such as *Story of Liu Yi*, *Story of Yingying*, *Story of Li Wa* and *Story of Huo Xiaoyu*; second, the emergence of storytellers' scripts in the Song Dynasty and the emergence of novels written in the style of storytellers' scripts in the Ming Dynasty promoted ancient novels' development; third, chapter-based novels of the Ming and Qing dynasties represented by *Romance of the Three Kingdoms*, *Water Margin*, *Journey to the West* and *Dream of the Red Chamber* pushed the development of ancient novels to the peak.

In terms of creation methods, Chinese ancient novels particularly focus on arrangement of stories and plots and depiction of characters and images. For example, the reason why *Romance of the Three Kingdoms* and *Water Margin* are widely known and highly influential is closely related to their legendary plots full of twists and turns and lifelike characters. Because novels were classified as "folk literature" for long in ancient China, targeting the class of ordinary citizens, most of them use language mixing classical Chinese and vernacular Chinese and contain vivid, specific and lifelike images.

Historical Novel
Romance of the Three Kingdoms

"The waters of the mighty Yangtzi flow eastward, its spray drowning countless heroes." Despite changes in time and space and the disappearance of the glint and flash of cold steel, the sky of history is still starry, colorful and lively. As a long historical novel, *Romance of the Three Kingdoms* vividly and fully presents a picture of heroes in troubled times. This long chapter-based novel with a length of 800,000 Chinese characters depicts a series of grand historical scenes and shapes numerous images of heroes of ideals and integrity against the backdrop of the political and military struggles in the late Eastern Han Dynasty and the Three Kingdoms Period. It is spread widely among people.

It is said that the author of *Romance of the Three Kingdoms* is Luo Guanzhong (c. 1330–c. 1400). He created this long novel on the basis of the historical book *Annals of the Three Kingdoms* written by Chen Shou (233–297) and stories of heroes spreading among people.

Romance of the Three Kingdoms mainly depicts the struggles among the three political and military groups of Wei, Shu and Wu, which exist relying on their heroic figures respectively. In the book, there are more than 1,200 characters with names, among whom the most influential ones are "the most legendary virtuous prime minister of all times" Zhuge Liang, "the most legendary famous general of all times" Guan Yu and "the most legendary capable but crafty person of all times" Cao Cao. There are also many other characters with unique personalities such as Lü Bu who is the bravest person in the army, Zhang Fei who is loyal but rash, Huang Zhong who is old but vigorous and Sima Yi who is shrewd and crafty.

Because the main ideological tendency of *Romance of the Three Kingdoms* is "supporting Liu and opposing Cao," characters of the Kingdom of Shu-Han are depicted in great detail. The most prominent civil character is Zhuge Liang, and the most prominent martial character is Guan Yu. Zhuge Liang assists Liu Bei and his son for 30 years, loyal to the throne, loving the people, totally devoted, having wonderful foresight and leaving much-told ancient tales such as "the Longzhong Plan," "borrowing arrows with thatched boats" and "the empty-city stratagem."

Guan Yu is reputed as a "military sage." After Liu Bei, Zhang Fei and he swear to be brothers in the peach garden, he follows Liu Bei to restore the Han Dynasty all his life. *In Romance of the Three Kingdoms*, Guan Yu's image is complex and three-dimensional: "slaying Hua Xiong before wine gets cold" shows his bravery, "passing through five check-points and slaying six generals" shows his loyalty, "allowing Cao Cao to pass through the Huarong Trail" shows his righteousness, "scraping the poison off the bone" shows his fortitude, and "fleeing to Mai in defeat" shows his self-conceit.

The Cao-Wei group is another main political and military group with Cao Cao as the main representative. On the one hand, he has great talent and bold vision, goes on a punitive expedition

Picture of Three Visits and One Encounter, painted by Sun Yi in the Qing Dynasty. This picture is based on the story of the three visits paid by Liu Bei to the thatched cottage to request Zhuge Liang to leave the mountain in *Romance of the Three Kingdoms*.

against Dong Zhuo, eliminates Yua Shao, has garrison troops or peasants open up wasteland, grow food grain and defend border areas, unites the north, "controls the emperor and commands the nobles;" on the other hand, he is crafty and cruel, feels no guilt for killing the whole family of his lifesaver Lü Boshe by mistake, and orders his troops to massacre all the residents in Xuzhou after capturing the city. "Better to wrong the world than have it wrong me" is his philosophy of life. In *Romance of the Three Kingdoms*, Cao Cao's image of a capable but crafty person is shown to the world.

In comparison, the Sun-Wu group in *Romance of the Three Kingdoms* is in a subordinate position in conflicts. Though the Wu Kingdom had numerous famous generals and outstanding talents such as Sun Jian, his sons Sun Ce and Sun Quan, Zhou Yu, Lu Su, Lü Meng and Lu Xun, the author adopted the attitude of belittling the emperors and ministers of the Wu Kingdom. For example, though Zhou Yu achieved his ambition in his early years and commanded the Sun-Wu allied forces to utterly defeat Cao Cao at the Red Cliff, he is narrow-minded and outwitted by Zhuge Liang, only leaving a sigh: "Zhou Yu has already been born, so why was Zhuge Liang ever born?"

Romance of the Three Kingdoms prominently shows the tendency of "supporting Liu and opposing Cao" because on the one hand Liu Bei is a member of the imperial family of the Han Dynasty and is "legitimate" according to Confucian views and on the other hand the Shu-Han group represents "benevolent governance." Liu Bei is a very fair and honest person and "would rather die than do anything ungrateful;" the core of his political thought is "benevolent governance" based on "people's support." Liu Bei has the air of a benevolent emperor. His fraternity with Guan Yu and Liu Bei and the emperor-minister relationship between him and Zhuge Liang and others constitute the Shu-Han Kingdom's "benevolent governance," which is the political paradigm eulogized in *Romance of the Three Kingdoms* with emphasis.

In terms of structures, *Romance of the Three Kingdoms* realized transition from biographical short legends of the Tang Dynasty to comprehensive long legends. The vertical structure developing according to the time order and the horizontal structure centering on contemporary characters' activities are mingled. In terms of language, the author of Romance of the Three Kingdoms drew on the experience of classical Chinese short novel creation. "Meanings are not profound, and words are not vulgar." It is elegant but not abstruse, smooth but not vulgar. Descriptions of characters and

Guan Yu is shot by a poisonous arrow, and the famous doctor Hua Tuo scrapes the poison off his bone. Guan Yu plays chess while recovering from the wound, talks and laughs naturally, showing his impressive heroic spirit.

objects are quite vivid and expressive, often manifesting their facial expressions in very few words. It is deeply loved by all people.

The turmoil in the troubled times attributed a unique martial quality to *Romance of the Three Kingdoms* as a historical novel depicting the Three Kingdoms Period. *Romance of the Three Kingdoms* unfolds against the backdrop of war from beginning to end. The author was very good at depicting war scenes and very good at depicting heroic figures under the environment of war such as Lü Bu fighting the three heroes, Guan Yu slaying Hua Xiong before wine gets cold, Zhang Fei shouting at the Changban Slope and Cao Cao composing poems while holding the lance horizontally in the saddle, using many methods including both direct narration and indirect description, both detailed depiction and simple sketching, and both depiction of reality with imagination and depiction of imagination with reality.

Meanwhile, the author also successfully handled the relationship between history and literature, and formed the artistic characteristic of "70% real and 30% imagined." While handling the relationship between historical facts and literary fictions, *Romance of the Three Kingdoms* sticks to the following main principles: first, they should be conducive to displaying characters' personalities more prominently; second, they should be conducive to making plots full of twists and turns, vivid and moving; third, they should comply with the whole book's overall political and moral tendency

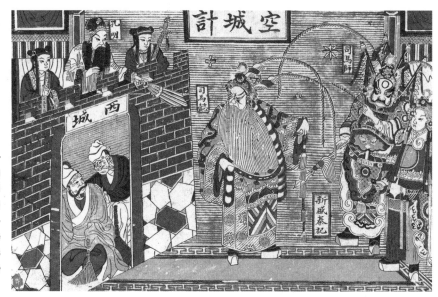

Spring Festival picture *Empty-city Stratagem*. Zhuge Liang is very resourceful, and intimidates the Wei army with an empty city. The "empty-city stratagem" is one of the most brilliant stratagems in *Romance of the Three Kingdoms*.

of "supporting Liu and abasing Cao." Such handling of the relationship between imagination and reality leads to the huge artistic impact and appeal of *Romance of the Three Kingdoms*, and turns it into a legend of heroes with far-reaching influence and an ode to people with lofty ideals.

Heroic Legend *Water Margin*

Ming (Rongyu Hall) block-printed edition of *Water Margin*

Shi Naian (c. 1296–1371), a contemporary of the author of *Romance of the Three Kingdoms*, created the long novel *Water Margin*, which depicts heroes, knights-errant, wicked people and robbers, includes funny parts and sad parts and encompasses all feelings in the world. It was handed down from the late Ming Dynasty to today, and its charm was everlasting.

Water Margin was the first chapter-based novel written in vernacular Chinese in China's history. With the theme of the Song Jiang Uprising in the late Northern Song Dynasty, it historically reproduces the occurrence, development course and tragic end of the uprising. In the Southern Song Dynasty, Liangshan heroes' stories were already widespread, and Gong Kai wrote *Eulogy of 36 Heroes Headed by Song Jiang and Preface in that period*. From the late Song Dynasty to the early Yuan Dynasty, many storytellers' scripts based on stories

of the Water Margin emerged. After interpretation in various dynasties, the number of Liangshan heroes in poetic drama of the Yuan Dynasty finally increased to 108.

Water Margin created by Shi Naian integrates the essence of previous stories of Liangshan heroes, keeps to the theme of "misgovernment driving people to revolt," and depicts a grand historical picture in detail. The spectacular heroic images shaped in *Water Margin* are most conspicuous. Shi Naian used multiple modes such as portrait description and detail description to vividly depict Liangshan heroes.

The 40th chapter is a dividing point in the book. The first 40 chapters mainly describe how various heroes gather at Liangshan. After the 40th chapter, the Liangshan Uprising develops to a new stage, and larger-scale combats with the government army and local despotic gentry's armed forces begin, such as the three attacks on Zhu Village, the capture of Zengtou Town, the capture of Gaotang and the attacks on Qingzhou, Huazhou, Daming Prefecture, Dongchang Prefecture, Dongping Prefecture, etc. Under the situation of the government army's consecutive setbacks, the imperial court begins to implement the policy of offering amnesty and enlistment to rebels. The Liangshan Uprising in *Water Margin* ends in thorough extermination after acceptance of the imperial court's amnesty and enlistment.

Majestic Star "Panther Head" Lin Chong is a complex image and a typical character "driven to revolt" in *Water Margin*. He is at first an upright and kindhearted martial arts instructor of the 800,000 imperial guards in Dongjing leading a relatively comfortable life and having no inordinate desire. Gao Qiu's son takes his wife by force and victimizes him. Lin Chong endures humiliation repeatedly and realizes he has no choice but to revolt when Gao Qiu, after one failed scheme, devises another one to kill him. So he kills his personal enemy and goes to Liangshan for shelter.

Leader Star "Protector of Justice" Song Jiang is called "Timely Rain" in the underworld. Having serving as an official for years, he is familiar with officialdom. On the one hand, he is generous in aiding needy people and good at leadership, and on the other hand, he is most ideologically loyal to the throne among the Liangshan heroes. Shi Naian vividly depicted this person with a complex personality. Today, the image of Song Jiang is still quite controversial among readers.

Shi Naian depicted characters' personalities vividly sometimes through language, sometimes through specific acts, sometimes through direct description, sometimes through deliberate digression for contrast and sometimes through few words. For example, Shi Naian describes "Pilgrim" Wu Song's countenance as "having two eyes like stars in the winter sky and two eyebrows like paint." Two eyes like stars in the winter sky alone reveal Wu Song's shrewd and valiant personality. Lin Chong, Lu Zhishen and Yang Zhi are all former military officers highly skilled in martial arts, but under Shi Naian's pen, their personalities are quite different. The Liangshan heroes in *Water Margin* have different charms and highlights, and can hardly be forgotten by readers.

Water Margin has a compound crisscross structure. The whole course of the Liangshan Uprising runs through the whole book, and is mingled with relatively independent characters and stories. *Water Margin* depicts characters vividly and depicts events more spectacularly. Stories such as Lin Chong's rush to Liangshan in a snowy night, Yang Zhi's sword sale, Wu Song's killing of a tiger and Lu Junyi's journey under escort were talked about with great relish in tens of hundreds of years. Wu Song's killing of a tiger is a famous story in *Water Margin*. Actually, there are three scenes of tiger-fighting in the book, i.e. Wu Song's killing of a tiger, Li Kui's slaying of tigers and Xie Zhen and Xie Bao's hunting of tigers. These three tiger-fighting scenes are not redundant at all, and these different heroes' personalities are fully demonstrated.

Excellent description of details is a great pioneering contribution of *Water Margin* to the art of Chinese ancient novels. *Romance of the Three Kingdoms* originated from "a historical book,"

Picture Scroll of Characters in Water Margin painted in the Qing Dynasty

so it focuses on macroscopic narration; *Water Margin* originated from "novels" so it excels in depiction, especially depiction of details. The depiction of Lin Chong in *Lin Chong Shelters from the Snowstorm in the Mountain Spirit Temple* is an example:

Entering, he shut the door and propped against it a big stone which he had noticed lying to one side. He walked further into the temple and saw on a platform an idol of a mountain spirit with golden armor, flanked by a Nether Region judge and a small demon, one on each side. In a corner was a pile of paper. Lin Chong inspected the whole temple but could find neither occupants nor anyone in charge. Lin placed his spear and gourd bottle on the pile of paper and untied his quilt. He removed his broad-brimmed felt hat, shook the snow from his clothes and peeled off his white tunic which was half soaked, then put it together with his hat on the altar table. He covered himself to the waist with the quilt and drank from the gourd bottle from time to time, helping the cold wine down with slices of the beef he had been carrying.

Spring Festival woodcut *Loyalty Hall* depicts the Liangshan heroes in the Loyalty Hall headed by Song Jiang.

Wu Song's Killing of a Tiger, painted by contemporary Liu Jiyou

Qing Spring Festival picture *Three Attacks on Zhu Village*

These few sentences depict Lin Chong's behavior after entry into the temple in great detail and depict the environment in the temple in a true and visible manner. The mild and slow tempo and the cold and solitary atmosphere "quietly" foreshadow the ensuing violent conflict.

Water Margin was the first long novel totally written in popular oral language in China's history, marking the maturity of ancient popular novels' linguistic art. In the course of description of people and depiction of concrete objects, the novel uses a lot of folk sayings and slang, making the overall linguistic style vivid, lively, clear and straightforward. Besides, the linguistic styles of characters in *Water Margin* are distinctive – for example, Song Jiang always talks about loyalty and righteousness, and Li Kui speaks rudely. Linguistic individualization plays an important role in shaping characters' images and pushing forward plot development.

Gods and Demons Novel
Journey to the West

"You carry the burden, I pull the horse. We welcome the sun as it rises, and bid goodbye as it sets. Stomp flat the bumpy road, to become the Great Way. After defeating dangers and obstacles, we set out again, and then again, from spring to summer and back again, through the **many** bouts of life's joys and sorrows. If you ask which **way to go**, the way is under your feet…" This is the theme **song** of the TV series *Journey to the West* widely known in China, vividly portraying the arduous and heroic journey of Tang Monk and his disciples to the West for fetching Buddhist scriptures from the Western Heaven.

Journey to the West, a gods and demons novel representing the highest accomplishments in the history of Chinese ancient literature, is said to be written by Wu Cheng'en (c. 1500–1582) in the Ming Dynasty. "Narration about gods and demons" is the most prominent artistic characteristic of *Journey to the West*. The characters in *Journey to the West* can be mainly classified into three categories: the first is immortals,

Sun Wukong in a shadow play

Buddhist figures and Taoist figures such as Gautama Buddha, Jade Emperor, Queen Mother of the West, Bodhisattva Guanyin, Most Exalted Lord Lao, God Erlang and Nezha; the second is mortals such as Emperor Taizong of the Tang Dynasty, Squire Kou and Marquis Shangguan; the third is monsters such as White Bone Spirit, Yellow Robe Monster, Great King of Miraculous Response, Bull Demon King, Red Boy and Scorpion Spirit. There are brilliant images with distinctive personalities in each category of characters.

Tang Monk is one of the most important characters in *Journey to the West*. He becomes a pious Buddhist with the monastic title of Xuanzang in his childhood. To benefit the country and all people, he leaves the Tang Dynasty's territory in the East to fetch Buddhist scriptures from the Western Heaven in spite of numerous difficulties and obstacles. On the way, he takes Sun Wukong, Zhu Bajie and Friar Sand as his disciples. Because of his adherence to the Buddhist rule of "having mercy and compassion," he gets into monsters' traps inadvertently several times. After experiencing 81 tribulations and overcoming numerous hardships and dangers, he finally obtains Buddhist scriptures and attains Buddhahood.

Sun Wukong is one of the most successful images shaped by Wu Cheng'en. He is originally a stone monkey formed by the coupling of Heaven and Earth. After mastering martial arts, he calls himself "Great Sage Equal to Heaven," solicits treasures from the Palace of the Dragon King, erases names in the Register of Life and Death, and creates havoc in Heaven, manifesting the rebellious spirit of resisting restraint, challenging authority, pursuing equality and emancipating personality in all aspects. This is the most prominent personal trait of Sun Wukong and the greatest charm of this image. Wu Cheng'en also described Sun Wukong's brave fight and resourcefulness in protecting Tang Monk on the road to the Western Heaven in a rich and colorful manner. With penetrating eyesight, he is capable of distinguishing truth from falsehood and is good at using the 72 methods of transformation and complicated conflicts to subdue demons.

Zhu Bajie is Tang Monk's second disciple with the monastic title of Wuneng. He is originally the Marshal of the Heavenly Canopy and is banished into the mortal world for getting drunk and flirting with Chang'e but ends up in the womb of a female boar due to are incarnation error. He is robust, strong, loyal and capable but fond of eating, averse to work and little lustful, and likes gaining petty advantages. Different from Tang Monk and Sun Wukong "having no interest in mundane affairs," the image of Zhu Bajie is a little secular and comical, deeply loved by people for long.

Still of TV series *Journey to the West*

The monsters raping women and plundering guilty of the worst crimes depicted in *Journey to the West* contrast sharply with Tang Monk and his disciples. These monsters occupy hills to act as lords and take advantage of power to bully people, representing evil forces in the society of that period. Meanwhile, these monsters have different shapes, backgrounds, abilities and means. White Bone Spirit is a typical representative among them. To eat Tang Monk's flesh and obtain immortality, White Bone Spirit transforms into a beautiful woman, an infirm old woman and a benign old man, but Sun Wukong sees through the disguise immediately no matter whom it transforms into. "Sun Wukong hitting White Bone Spirit thrice" is also a classic story in *Journey to the West*.

The overall keynote of *Journey to the West* is magical, but the reality it refers to is true and profound. The author did not intend to expose the dark side of the society directly, but the objective effect was "conveying secrets in games." In the author's jeers, sarcasms and jokes, the social malpractices of that period and people disregarding law and discipline, taking advantage of power to bully people and living in extreme luxury are satirized ruthlessly. This is the realistic significance of the gods and demons novel *Journey to the West* different from ordinary novels.

In terms of the structure, *Journey to the West* consists of a total of 100 chapters, and their contents can be classified into three parts: Chapters 1-7 describe the birth of the stone monkey and havoc in Heaven; Chapters 8-12 describe the reason why Tang Monk wants to fetch Buddhist scriptures from the Western Heaven; Chapters 13-100 describe the arduous journey of Monk Tang to the Western Heaven under the protection of Sun Wukong, Zhu Bajie and Friar Sand. These three parts form an organic whole. The first and third are the key parts and the second one is mainly for plot transition.

As a gods and demons novel, "magic" and "imagination" constitute the main artistic characteristics of *Journey to the West*. The first one is "magic." *Journey to the West* conceives a series of bizarre and magnificent scenes with not only a sense of reality, but also a sense of strangeness and vividness particular to the world of gods and demons. The author described various infinitely resourceful gods and various treasures with boundless supernatural power. Each story is full of ups and downs with clear causes and effects, and the scenes are surprisingly beautiful and eccentric. The Mountain of Flowers and Fruit is a magical scene depicted by the author:

This country is next to an ocean, and in the middle of the ocean is a famous island called the Mountain of Flowers and Fruit. This mountain is the ancestral artery of the Ten Continents, the origin of the Three Islands; it was formed when the clear and impure were separated and the Enormous Vagueness was divided...

Red cliffs and strange rocks;
Beetling crags and jagged peaks.
On the red cliffs phoenixes sing in pairs;
Lone unicorns lie before the beetling crags.
The cry of pheasants is heard upon the peaks;
In caves the dragons come and go.
There are deer of long life and magic foxes in the woods;

Picture Book of Journey to the West, painted in the Ming Dynasty

Spring Festival picture *Bottomless Abyss* depicts the scene of Sun Wukong and Nezha fighting the Jade Mouse Ogre.

Miraculous birds and black cranes in the trees.
There are flowers of jade and strange plants that wither not;
Green pine and bluish cypress ever in leaf,
Magic peaches always in fruit.
Clouds gather round the tall bamboo.
The wisteria grows thick around the mountain brook
And the banks around are newly-colored with flowers.
It is the Heaven-supporting pillar where all the rivers meet,
The Earth's root, unchanged through a myriad aeon.

The other artistic charm of *Journey to the West* is "imagination," i.e. its strong imaginative power. Because it is a fantasy novel on gods and demons, abundant imagination is necessary for organization of plots and shaping of characters' images. *In Journey to the West*, Sun Wukong, Zhu Bajie, Dragon King and numerous monsters are all images invented by the author. The author also imagined magical scenes such as infinite stretching of the gold-bound staff, the fight between the real and fake Monkey King and the 81 tribulations.

Of course, *Journey to the West* has shortcomings in ideological contents and artistic accomplishments. For example, in terms of thoughts, it has a strong sense of fate and reincarnation; in terms of plot designs, sometimes its description of all the 81 tribulations shows a redundant tendency. In terms of depiction of characters, the images of Tang Monk, Friar Sand, Jade Emperor, etc. are relatively insubstantial and their personalities are not demonstrated sufficiently. Among the numerous immortals, Buddhist figures, Taoist figures and monsters, few have really prominent personalities and deeply impress people.

Ghost Novel Strange Stories from a Chinese Studio

In the 17th century, a glorious romantic ghost novel emerged in China. It spread widely in the form of hand-written copies at first, was performed on the stage of traditional Chinese opera later, and now has been adapted to films and TV series deeply loved by people. This is *Strange Stories from a Chinese Studio*, a collection of short novels written in classical Chinese in the Qing Dynasty. Its author was Pu Songling (1640–1715), a native of Zibo, Shandong, called Mr. Liaozhai by people after the name of his studio.

Strange Stories from a Chinese Studio (*A Chinese Studio* for short) is usually called *Stories of Ghosts and Foxes* consisting of 12 chapters and 491 stories with diversified contents on a wide range of themes. Most works in the book are stories about spirits, monsters, ghosts and goblins. The book recording strange stories is named after the name of the author's

Figure of Pu Songling

studio. Pu Songling created *Strange Stories from a Chinese Studio* on the basis of extensively gathering folk ghost stories, unofficial history and miscellaneous talks.

Many works in *A Chinese Studio* expose the dark reality of the feudal society and reflect corrupt officials' atrocities of taking bribes, perverting justice and tyrannizing people. Representatives of such works mainly include *Xi Fangping, Dream of Wolves, The Cricket*, etc. *Xi Fangping* describes the miserable experiences of the family of Xi Lian and Xi Fangping. Because the grudge between Xi Lian and Yang from a rich family in the village, Yang bribes officials in the afterworld after death and causes Xi Lian to die in injustice. Xi Lian's son Xi Fangping knows his father's death in injustice very well, so he appeals for justice in the afterworld. However, Yang continues to bribe officials in the afterworld and buys over the king of the afterworld. They torture Xi Fangping cruelly, but Xi Fangping is always firm and unyielding and never gives in.

The imperial examination system born in the Sui and Tang dynasties was already full of abuses in the Ming and Qing dynasties. Pu Songling had an in-depth understanding of this. He was well-read in the Book of Songs and the Book of History, knowledgeable and very creative, but he failed in many imperial examinations while those dandies smoothly became officials through bribing examiners. The cruel social reality made Pu Songling extremely disappointed about the imperial examination system, so he wrote a series of works represented by *The Bureau of Examination Frauds, The Certifier of Articles, Scholar Ye, Ghost-Scholar Yu Qu-E, Jia Fengzhi* and *Scholar Wang Zi-An* to expose and satirize the dark side of the feudal imperial examination system. In *The Certifier of Articles*, a blind monk can smell whether an article is good or bad, so Wang Pingzi asks him to authenticate his article. After smelling the article, the blind monk says Wang Pingzi is highly accomplished and can pass the examination. After some time, Yu Hangsheng consults the blind monk, and the blind monk judges he cannot pass the examination. However, the list of successful candidates released after several days includes Yu Hangsheng but not Wang Pingzi. The blind monk sighs with emotion, "Though my eyes are blind, my nose is not," but the chief examiner's eyes and nose are both blind. This is undoubtedly a biting satire on the imperial examination system.

"Love is man's eternal theme." Works eulogizing pure love are most numerous in *Strange Stories from a Chinese Studio*. These works boldly eulogize beautiful love between young men and women and express discontent with feudal marriage, represented by *Lotus Fragrance, Fragrant Jade, Yingning*, etc. *Fragrant Jade* describes the story of the acquaintance and love between Huang

Sheng and a peony spirit. The white peony passionately loved by Huang Sheng dies after being removed. Feeling extremely sad, Huang Sheng writes 50 poems and complains in tears day and night. Unexpectedly, the white peony revives, but Huang Sheng becomes a peony staying beside the white peony day and night. The author passionately eulogized such true love "startling the universe and moving the gods."

In the vast Chinese ancient literature, *Strange Stories from a Chinese Studio* with its unique artistic charm has a style of its own. The most prominent aspect is that its expression methods are novel and special. The work reflects real life of that period through unreal stories of flower and fox spirits. Most of these flower and fox spirits "have human feelings," with not only the features of their natural archetypes, but also human emotions. There are many flower and fox spirits in *Strange Stories from a Chinese Studio*. The author's general attitude towards them is in favor of them. Many fox spirits have beautiful faces and graceful postures with the characters of innocence, kindheartedness, bravery and wisdom.

Most stories in *Strange Stories from a Chinese Studio* have plots full of twists and turns. Lu Xun's evaluation is "recording strange stories by means of legends." the so-called "means of legends" refers to legends' "great momentum and flowery language," making stories' plots full of twists and turns, making narrations more exciting and making writing techniques more mature. In terms of language, words used in *Strange Stories from a Chinese Studio* are subtle and refined. Oral language, slang and the Shandong dialect are often introduced, making the overall linguistic style vivid, elegant, unconventional and very expressive in terms of description of people and depiction of concrete objects.

There are more than 400 stories in total and no less than 100 vivid characters with distinctive personalities, especially many lovely women's images, in *Strange Stories from a Chinese Studio*. Some of them are fox spirits, some are flower spirits, some are affectionate, and some have strong emotions, giving out charming fragrance and touching glory. For example, the fox spirit Xiaocui is warmhearted and outgoing, Qing Feng is shy and clever, Yingning is simple and honest, Bai Qiulian is elegant…

When talking about the reason why he created *Strange Stories from a Chinese Studio*, Pu Songling said, "I sew together the finest fragments of fox fur to make a fur coat and want to

The Cricket tells the story of an ordinary family's overwhelming joy and sorrow from offering crickets as tribute to the imperial court.

Painted Skin tells the story of a malicious ghost in human skin disguised as a beautiful woman and eating people.

continue *Records of the Hidden and the Visible Worlds*; I drink wine with a big cup to write a book similar to Solitary Indignation. Such hope makes me feel very sad!" Though he never achieved his ambition in his lifetime, his *Strange Stories from a Chinese Studio* was widely spread among people and highly evaluated by later scholars. Modern writer Lao She praised this book, saying "ghosts and fox have personalities, and jokes and reproaches form essays;" Guo Moruo also highly praised this book, saying "ghosts and spirits are depicted better than others and corruption and brutality are satirized bitterly."

Masterpiece Dream of the Red Chamber

After nearly one thousand years of development, *Dream of the Red Chamber*, the masterpiece among Chinese classical novels, emerged in the 18th century.

Dream of the Red Chamber is also known as *The Story of the Stone*. After its emergence, it spread in the form of hand-written copies for several decades. "At that time, hardworking people sold each hand-written copy on the market at the price of dozens of tales of gold, and it spread far and wide!" At that time, there was also a saying, "If one does not talk about *Dream of the Red Chamber*, he has read *the Book of Songs* and *the Book of History* in vain."

The most widely known stories in *Dream of the Red Chamber* are the love story of Jia Baoyu and Lin Daiyu and the story of the decline of the influential Jia, Wang, Shi and Xue families. The book consists of 120 chapters. It is generally thought that the first 80 chapters were written by Cao Xueqin and that the last 40 chapters were written by Gao E.

Figure of Cao Xueqin, painted by contemporary Jiang Zhaohe

Cao Xueqin, with the given name of Zhan and the alias of Xueqin, was born in Jiangning Prefecture (today's Nanjing) around 1715 and died around 1763 in the Qing Dynasty. His ancestor served as Commissioner of Imperial Textiles in Jiangning, and he went through the course of his family's quick decline, experienced the sudden change in the feudal dynasty's political environment and felt social snobbery and inconstancy of human relationships. After his family declined, he led a wretched life and "the whole family often bought porridge and wine on credit." Therefore, he had a special deep understanding of society and life. Cao Xueqin used to say, "Pages full of fantastic talk penned with bitter tears; all men call the author mad, none his messages hears." *All Good Things Must End* in *Dream of the Red Chamber* vividly describes such changes in world affairs and extremes of fortune:

All men long to be immortals,
Yet to riches and rank each aspires;
The great ones of old, where are they now?
Their graves are a mass of briars.
All men long to be immortals,
Yet silver and gold they prize.
And grub for money all their lives,
Till death seals up their eyes.
All men long to be immortals
Yet dote on the wives they've wed,
Who swear to love their husband evermore,
But remarry as soon as he's dead.
All men long to be immortals,
Yet with getting sons won't have done.
Although fond parents are legion,
Who ever saw a really filial son?

This just reveals the decline of the four families and the inevitability of such decline. In *Dream of the Red Chamber*, description follows the main line of the Ning mansion's decline. This distinguished Jia family impressive in appearance has numerous hidden problems. If we analyze the reasons for the Jia family's decline, the direct reason is none other than Concubine Yuan's death. As a result, the Jia family loses favor, is squeezed by people in power and is raided. However, the fundamental reasons are as follows: first, the Jia family's children have no initiative or drive, waste money at will, seek Taoist immortality, and stubbornly adhere to outworn rules and ideas; second, they are imperious and despotic like Wang Xifeng, and often extort money by blackmail and kill for money; third, the whole Jia family is full of conflicts. As Tanchun says, "We must start killing each other first before our family can be completely destroyed."

The most thrilling story in *Dream of the Red Chamber* is the love tragedy of Jia Baoyu and Lin Daiyu, which is a tragedy of fate, of personality and of the society of that period. Firstly, the tragedy of Jia Baoyu and Lin Daiyu is a tragedy of fate. The love between Jia Baoyu and Lin Daiyu

Selected from *The Illustrated Complete Dream of the Red Chamber*, painted by Sun Wen in the Qing Dynasty. This picture shows the plot that Baoyu throws jade to the ground after meeting Daiyu for the first time in Chapter 3 of Dream of *the Red Chamber.*

seems predestined by the deeply moving "pledge between plant and stone," but fate plays tricks because the saying of "well-matched gold and jade" emerges. Facing the "pledge between plant and stone" and "well-matched gold and jade," though Jia Baoyu has a liking for Lin Daiyu, he is tiny in front of the feudal ethical codes. This is also the fate of Jia Baoyu as the only heir of the Jia family's children who can possibly revive the family. Therefore, elder members of the family must destroy the love between Jia Baoyu and Lin Daiyu and must choose Xue Baochai who supports feudalism as his wife. Besides, the troubled Jia family also longs for the Xue family's support and urgently needs the capable Xue Baochai to run the family. The "well-matched gold and jade" reflect the Jia and Xue families' fundamental interests. Jia Baoyu and Lin Daiyu can hardly escape such fate.

Secondly, it is a tragedy of personality. Daiyu "looks more sensitive than Pi Gan." While living in the Jia family, "she must watch her step in her new home, she decided, be on guard every moment and weigh every word, so as not to be laughed at for any foolish blunder." However, though Daiyu depends on other people for a living, she is proud and aloof by nature, innocent,

Picture of Nocturnal Birthday Revels of Flower-maidens, painted in the Qing Dynasty, shows the plot that various sisters celebrate Baoyu's birthday in Chapter 63 of *Dream of the Red Chamber*.

Daiyu Weeping Over Fallen Blossoms, painted by Fei Danxu in the Qing Dynasty

straightforward, artless and clearly aware of whom to love and whom to hate, making no attempt to conceal her pleasure, anger, likes and dislikes. The poem *Weeping Over Fallen Blossoms* is the best picture of Daiyu:

I long to take wing and fly
With the flowers to earth's uttermost bound;
And yet at earth's uttermost bound
Where can a fragrant burial mound be found?
Better shroud the fair petals in silk
With clean earth for their outer attire;
For pure you came and pure shall you go,
Not sinking into some foul ditch or mire.
Now you are dead I come to bury you;
None has divined the day when I shall die;
Men laugh at my folly in burying fallen flowers,
But who will bury me when dead I lie?
See, when spring draws to a close and flowers fall,
This is the season when beauty must ebb and fade;
The day that spring takes wing and beauty fades
Who will care for the fallen blossom or dead maid?

"For pure you came and pure shall you go" is just her pursuit of character. She never flatters the rulers in the Jia family to curry favor with them. Because of her poor family background and strong self-esteem, Daiyu is particularly sensitive to others' discrimination and ridicule. Based on the self-defense psychology, Daiyu sometimes says bitterly sarcastic words and sometimes cries, giving people the impression that she "loses her temper like a child." Such temperament and temper can hardly let her integrate into the complex and big Jia family and, on the contrary, aggravate others' prejudice against her.

As to Jia Baoyu, the author made a general and vivid explanation in Chapter 3: "Absurdly

he courts care and melancholy and raves like any madman in his folly; for though endowed with handsome looks is he, his heart is lawless and refractory. Too dense by far to understand his duty, too stubborn to apply himself to study, foolhardy in his eccentricity, he's deaf to all reproach and obloquy." The most distinctive personality attributed to Jia Baoyu by the author is the rebellious spirit out of tune with the society of that period. He is discontent with, disgusted by and even resentful of the life of extravagance, ease and glory, and refuses to take the road of "pursuing studies to become officials" taken by most children of aerostatic families. He boldly challenges the concept of male domination and female subordination, and places all his passions and ideals on those innocent girls. Lin Daiyu happens to be his ideologically intimate friend. He declares in public, "Has Miss Lin ever talked such disgusting nonsense? If she had, I'd have stopped having anything to do with her long ago." This shows the side out of tune with feudal thoughts in the personalities of Jia Baoyu and Lin Daiyu. As a result, they cannot be possibly permitted by the feudal society to love.

Lastly, it is a tragedy of society. The two protagonist lovers in *Dream of the Red Chamber* Jia Baoyu and Lin Daiyu are no longer a talented man and a beautiful woman often depicted in previous dramas and novels but two persons who have eccentric personalities, are ridiculed by others as "idiots" and rebel against feudalism. This tragedy is caused by the impossibility of free courtship in the society of that period as well as shackles of many ideological and living problems. For example, male domination and female subordination in feudal families, master-servant relationships, ethical codes, moralities, etc. are all the whole society's problems that cannot be possibly resisted by Jia Baoyu and Lin Daiyu as rebellious people alone. Therefore, what causes the tragedy is not simple unmatched social and economic status or free courtship violating the feudal marriage system but the social intolerance of the anti-feudal color in the love itself. This fundamentally determines the tragic end of the love between Jia Baoyu and Lin Daiyu.

Dream of the Red Chamber excels in storytelling, and the artistic methods used in it, especially the art of language, striking everyone with admiration. First, characters' dialogues are especially brilliant. Characters' dialogues in *Dream of the Red Chamber* have not only the function of depiction of characters, but also the function of narration, theme revelation and personality summarization. Words that seem flat and implicit contain deep connotations, making people feel as if they can hear the sound clearly. For example, when Wang Xifeng appears, "her sound is heard

Still of TV series *Dream of the Red Chamber*

before she is seen." Her status as a capable and experienced housekeeper saying artful words and having insinuating countenance is revealed at once. Second, words are expressive, precise and to the point. This is fully manifested in *Dream of the Red Chamber*: words are clear, coherent, very meaningful, extremely concise and diversified. Its wording and phrasing even reach the state of "no possible word change, no possible word addition or deletion and empathy." Third, the language in *Dream of the Red Chamber* has a kind of plain beauty containing a strong poetic quality. Those beautiful poems add an infinite poetic flavor, poeticizing life, environment and characters' feelings and personalities. Plain and poetic language makes *Dream of the Red Chamber* reach the artistic state of suiting both refined and popular tastes.

Dream of the Red Chamber not only belongs to China, but also to the world. There are abridged translations and complete translations in more than ten languages including English, French and Russian, many foreigners study it, and many works about it have been written. *Dream of the Red Chamber* has become the whole world's common spiritual wealth.

Overview of the Development of Chinese Modern and Contemporary Literature

Chinese new literature with the "May 4th" Movement as the beginning is usually divided into the two stage of the modern era and the contemporary era. Modern literature began with the "literary revolution" that occurred around 1917 and ended with the founding of the People's Republic of China in 1949; contemporary literature refers to literature since 1949. Though modern literature has a history of only about 30 years, it is a huge and fundamental turning point in the development course of Chinese literature with the historical quality of a connecting link between the preceding and the following like no other period of Chinese literature history. Contemporary literature underwent a complicated and changeful course of development. It is becoming closer and closer to social life and opening to the outside world like never before.

Historical Course of Chinese Modern and Contemporary Literature

Three Decades of Modern Literature's Development

The first decade (1917–1927) is the stage of expansion and foundation of modern literature. A number of founders of modern literature such as Lu Xun and Guo Moruo, their foundation works and a number of important literary groups and schools such as the Literary Research Society and the Creation Society all emerged in this stage. At the beginning of 1917, Hu Shi and Chen Duxiu published *Some Modest Proposals for the Reform of Literature* and *On Literary Revolution* in *New Youth*, marking the beginning of the Literary Revolution Movement. Later a lot of literary publications and new literary societies emerged. Important ones among them included the Literary Research Society, the Creation Society, the Yusi Society and the Crescent Society. The Literary Research Society's pursuit of realism and the Creation Society's praise of romanticism formed two stylistic schools with unique characteristics and exerted profound influence on the development of new literature. New literary writers in this period also translated a lot of foreign literary works, and expanded the link between Chinese literature and world literature.

New Youth was the main front of advocating "new culture" and "new literature."

The second decade (1928–1937) is the stage of development and maturation of modern literature. The Proletarian Revolutionary Literature Movement further enhanced the relationship between literature and society. Leftist literary groups such as the "League of Leftist Writers" established in early 1930s pushed this movement to the climax. The ideological and social contents in the literary works created in this period were enhanced significantly, and writers reflected and exposed imperialist countries' military, economic and cultural invasion of China from various aspects and criticized the grotesque, variegated, extravagant and decadent life in the semi-colonial and semi-feudal society. Many writers not only manifested the miserable experiences of people at the bottom of the society and focused on describing their awakening and resistance, demonstrating the new ideological depth reached by new literary creations.

The third decade (1938–1949) is the stage of deepening and transformation of modern literature. The outbreak of the War of Resistance against Japan and the ongoing War of Liberation made national and class struggles the main contents of literature in this period, which is divided into two stages with 1942 as the dividing point. The first stage is literature of the early period of the War of Resistance against Japan, and resisting Japan and saving the nation from extinction is the overriding literary theme. A lot of popular, lively, short and concise literary works such as street poems and one-act plays emerged. Meanwhile, a series of historical dramas also emerged, and writers all manifested the daunting reality and expressed people's righteous calls through historical stories. Among them, *Qu Yuan*, *Tiger-shaped Tally*, etc. by Guo Moruo were most influential. Literature of the second stage can be classified into literature of the liberated region and literature of the Kuomintang-ruled region. In the liberated region, Mao Zedong proposed the direction of serving workers, peasants and soldiers with literature and art and emphasized the Chinese styles and national characteristics of literature in *Talks at the Yan'an Forum on Literature and Art*. In the Kuomintang-ruled region, the themes of literary creations were opposing oppression and striving for democracy, and a lot of satirical and revelatory works emerged, such as *Corrosion* by Mao Dun, *Cold Night* by Ba Jin, *Folk Song of Ma Fantuo* by Yuan Shuipai, *The Picture of Promotion in Officialdom* by Chen Baichen and *Fortress Besieged* by Qian Zhongshu. Writers exposed and criticized the dark reality in the Kuomintang-ruled region from different aspects by using different styles.

Four Stages of Contemporary Literature's Development

The literature of 17 years (1949–1965) is the first stage of literature after the founding of the People's Republic of China. It inherited the new literary traditions since the "May 4th" Movement, and advocated socialist realistic creation methods. Its basic features were: literature entered a new historical stage, and all writers very passionately eulogized the new society, depicted the new era when the people were the masters of the country, showed the great social changes, and manifested the socialist spirit of the times.

Literature of the "Cultural Revolution" period (1966–1976) is literature of this specific historical period. Great social turbulences and damages brought unprecedented disasters to literature. During the "Cultural Revolution," though some literary works were created, political ideas and intentions were more directly transformed into literary works, and a specific political meaning was attributed to the acceptance of works. Literature was thoroughly distorted in this period.

Literature of the new period (1977–1995): Literature revived and prospered with the ideological emancipation and social development from the end of the "Cultural Revolution" to the beginning of reform and opening up and 1992 when China began to implement the socialist market economy. Literary and artistic thoughts and literary creation were both very active in this period, and literary themes, forms and styles were diversified. Apart from the realistic trend, the literary thoughts, schools and creation methods of various countries in the world such as symbolism, the stream of consciousness, surrealism, hallucinatory realism, the absurdist school and black humor were almost all reflected by writers, manifesting the bold, exploratory and innovative spirit of writers of the new period.

Literature at the turn of the century (1996–now): With economic globalization and IT application in people's life, the development of literature also entered the new stage of diversification and coexistence of cultural forms and cultural views. Many writers stick to integrating individual styles and national spirit, actively exploring forms of artistic expression and constantly tapping ideological depths. The Nobel Prize in Literature won by Mo Yan marks a new height of Chinese contemporary literature. Meanwhile, the emergence of writers born in 1980s and 1990s and the rapid development of Internet literature also herald new prospects and challenges facing Chinese contemporary literature.

Main Characteristics of Chinese Modern and Contemporary Literature

Essential Characteristics of Modern Literature

As a link between the preceding and the following, modern literature has salient essential characteristics:

Conflict between new and old literature and inheritance.

Modern literature emerged under the new historical conditions during the "May 4th" Movement, reflecting the brand new modern society, modern life's spiritual outlook and brand new modes of literary expression, but it was also the inevitable result of Chinese traditional literature's development and evolvement in thousands of years. For example, Chinese novels have a long history and numerous vernacular novels emerged in the Ming and Qing dynasties, but modern novels written after the "May 4th" Movement opened a brand new chapter in the history of Chinese novels' development with brand new ideological connotations and unprecedented forms of expression, showing modern people's behavioral modes and thinking modes. However, the ideological essence and artistic techniques of Chinese traditional novels were still inherited by modern novels invisibly but in depth. The same goes for poetry. New poetry was established in a revolt against and complete break from traditional old poetry, but traditional poetry's aesthetic conceptions and classical poets' aesthetic accomplishments, especially Chinese classical poetry's traditional spirit of experiencing the times, worrying about the people and detesting the ways of the world exerted great influence on modern poets at a deep level.

Blending of Chinese and foreign literature.

Modern literature developed on the basis of fully absorbing various foreign countries' culture and literature, and many new cultural writers' works even emerged under the directly influence of foreign literature. This characteristic of "May 4th" new literature made it fundamentally different from Chinese traditional literature of the previous thousands of years. The formation of Chinese new literature was closely associated with the impact of the world's literary trend. Modern new poetry emerged under the collision with and stimulation of foreign cultural thoughts to a large extent. Those foreign critical realistic and romantic writers' works and those free and open ideological pursuits and artistic forms just complied with the historical tasks of "May 4th" new literature and brought about the emergence of Chinese modern new poetry.

Always having a sense of mission and a sense of responsibility.

Though modern literature did not have a long history, but numerous masters, famous works and schools of creation with unique styles emerged. In 30 years, a number of highly accomplished writers such as Lu Xun, Guo Moruo, Mao Dun, Ba Jin, Lao She, Cao Yu, Ai Qing, Ding Ling, Zhao Shuli, Ye Shengtao, Xu Dishan, Zhu Ziqing, Zhou Zuoren, Hu Shi, Bing Xin, Wen Yiduo, Xu Zhimo, Dai Wangshu, Mu Dan, Xiao Hong, Shen Congwen, Qian Zhongshu and Zhang Ailing emerged. This can only be called a special gift of the times and history for modern literature. Modern literature generally formed its fundamental characteristic, i.e. a sense of responsibility, a sense of mission and constant pursuit of the artistic state. This characteristic led to Chinese modern literature's attainment of a very high ideological level and artistic level.

Main Characteristics of Contemporary Literature

After many ups and downs, contemporary literature kept developing forward and formed its important characteristics in this course.

Literature and the times were closely associated.

Contemporary literature inherited the essence of "May 4th" new literature, and the times attributed to it a salient socialist quality, which determines that contemporary literature is always influenced by the times and society in the course of its development. Reflecting the themes of the times, showing social progress and manifesting people's spiritual outlook are the basic appeals of modern literature.

The singular literary pattern was diversified.

With the continuous development of the times and society, contemporary literature also evolved from the singular pattern to diversification. From literature of workers, peasants and soldiers to realism, modernism and postmodernism, etc., contemporary literature gradually eliminated the restrictive thought that literature should serve politics, and brought about evolution of literary concepts and values. Reference and exploration occurred repeatedly, and different styles and schools contended, and the literary circles showed an increasingly open pattern.

Exploration and bewilderment coexisted.

In today's era of globalization and IT application, various cultural differences and cultural conflicts also gradually emerged. After 1990s, the conflict between literary creation and commercial operation was increasingly intense. Under the market system, pure literature and popular literature could not be separated from publication and choice of the cultural consumption market. Writers' and intellectuals' roles and positions in the whole society were increasingly "marginalized," so in the contents expressed by modern literature, optimism was weakened to a large extent, hesitation, bewilderment, criticism and self-reflection were highlighted, and the characteristic of coexistence of exploration and bewilderment was formed.

Modern Novels: Echoes of the Times

The earliest modern novels are short ones. During the "May 4th" Movement, realistic creations represented by Ye Shengtao and romantic creations represented by Yu Dafu were mostly short works. Lu Xun was very good at writing short and concise novels. The epoch-making work *A Madman's Diary* and later collections *Call to Arms and Wandering* featuring diversified methods and styles can be called the peak of modern short novels. Around the 1930s, more and more medium-length and long novels emerged, and *Midnight* by Mao Dun, *The Family* by Ba Jin, *Rickshaw Boy* by Lao She, *Border Town* by Shen Congwen, etc. pushed modern novels to a mature state. In the 1940s and 1950s, long novels developed constantly, and both new and old writers published successful works such as *Cold Night* by Ba Jin, *Four Generations under One Roof* by Lao She, *Fortress Besieged* by Qian Zhongshu, *The Sun Shines Over Sanggan River* by Ding Ling, *The Hurricane* by Zhou Libo, *Red Crag*, *Red Sun*, *Keep the Red Flag Flying*, *Song of Youth*, etc. In the "Cultural Revolution" period, the long novels *Sunny* and *Golden Road* created by Haoran became typical works of that period.

Lu Xun: Founder of New Literature

Lu Xun

Lu Xun, with the original name of Zhou Shuren, was born in a declining scholar-bureaucrat's family. "Lu Xun" is the pen name used by him for the first vernacular novel *A Madman's Diary* published by him. In his youth, he studied in an old-style private school, took an imperial examination, and was well grounded in traditional culture. In 1898, he left home to pursue new learning in Nanjing and other places. From 1902 to 1909, he studied in Japan. In this period, he increasingly realized that it was more important to cure Chinese people's spiritual ills rather than their physical diseases, so he abandoned his medical career and selected literature as his path of saving Chinese people's spirit.

Lu Xun published China's first modern vernacular novel *A Madman's Diary* in *New Youth* in May 1918, later published more than ten novels including *Kong Yiji*, *Medicine* and *The True Story of Ah Q* successively, and published the collection *Call to Arms* in 1923. These works revealed the actual achievements of the literary revolution, deeply shook young intellectuals pursuing progress then, and laid a foundation for the development of Chinese modern novels with thorough and profound anti-feudal thoughts and novel and mature artistic forms. Later, Lu Xun successively created and published the novel collection *Wandering*, the lyric prose collection *Wild Grass*, the narrative prose collection *Dawn Blossoms Plucked at Dusk*, the historical novel collection *Old Tales Retold* and more than ten essay collections. All of Lu Xun's literary creations and literary activities were for one lofty goal, i.e. reforming Chinese people's spirit and saving the destiny of the nation. It was the origin of the greatness and profoundness of Lu Xun's works and his thoughts. In October 1936, Lu Xun died of illness in Shanghai. His coffin was covered by a flag sewn with the words "National Soul."

Lu Xun's manuscript

Cover of *Call to Arms* designed by Lu Xun himself

Initial Call: *A Madman's Diary*

A Madman's Diary is the first vernacular novel written by Lu Xun and the first short novel in the true modern sense in the history of new literature. Through the method of combining reality and symbols, the novel reveals profound contents at three levels through the madman's stream of

consciousness: first, seeing through the madman's eyes that China's history of thousands of years was "man-eating" history; second; showing through the madman's feelings that man-eating existed not only in history, but also in reality; third, shouting "save the children" through the madman's mouth and expressing future expectations. The image of the "madman" is not only vivid, but also of special symbolic significance. He is a symbol of the group of advanced intellectuals including Lu Xun who awakened earliest during the "May 4th" Movement.

Immortal Famous Work: *The True Story of Ah Q*

The True Story of Ah Q was first published in the *Beijing Morning News* supplement as a serial from December 1921 to February 1922.

The protagonist in the novel Ah Q lives in Wei Village, a village in the middle and lower reaches of the Yangtze River suffering deep social conflicts during the Revolution of 1911. He is a very poor vagrant farmhand with no home, no job, no relative and no friend, making a living by doing short-term work for others. People in Wei Village do not give attention to Ah Q normally, and only remember this cheap laborer when they are busy. Ah Q's social status is very low. He even does not know his family name. Once he says he is a namesake of landlord Zhao after drinking two cups of yellow wine, and landlord Zhao sends a town crier to summon him, slaps him in the face and prohibits him from having the surname Zhao. Ah Q's spirit and character are ridiculed and harmed by people from time to time. However, such a humiliated and harmed person seems to have no real worry himself and, to the contrary, leads a life of ease and leisure. This is because Ah Q is restricted by a horrible spiritual shackle, which is the "spiritual victory method:" whenever he is humiliated in

Figure of Ah Q, painted by Jiang Zhaohe

life, he comforts himself with "witty remarks" such as "who do you think you are anyway" and "it is as if I were beaten by my son," "defeats" his enemy in imagination, and eliminates humiliation through self-deception to get comfort; he is excessively concerned about face-saving, dare not directly face his weaknesses and shortcomings, and considers it "a great loss of face" to have less lice than Whiskers Wang; he bullies kindhearted people and fears evil people. He dare not fight after landlord Zhao slaps him in the face and after the Imitation Foreign Devil beats him with a mourner's stick, but he retaliates against weak ones. His teasing of a young nun and his fighting with Whiskers Wang and Young D are typical manifestations. Besides, Ah Q is also very numb and forgetful. No matter how greatly he is humiliated, he can, after obtaining "spiritual victory," make his way cheerfully to the wine shop to drink a few bowls of wine, joke with the others again, and return cheerfully to the temple he lives in, there to fall asleep as soon as his head touched the pillow.

Ah Q's "spiritual victory method" was a social mental morbidity. Lu Xun's analysis of it was intended to criticize the whole old society. Lu Xun said many times that the actual purpose of shaping the image of Ah Q was to depict Chinese people's souls and save the nation's destiny. Ah Q was "the soul of modern Chinese people." Ah Q's tragic fate shows in depth: only through powerful ideological enlightenment and thorough elimination of Chinese people's spiritual shackles could China's democratic revolution have bright prospects.

The artistic achievements of *The True Story of Ah Q* are reflected in many aspects. First, artistic descriptions are very typical. The novel adopts the typical character shaping method of "combing several characters into one," showing a high degree of generality. The novel purposefully downplays the characteristics of Ah Q's status, describes him as a link between various social classes and even between urban and rural areas, and thus enhances the general applicability of the "Ah Q mentality" to Chinese people of that period. Wei Village can also be regarded as an epitome of ancient China. Such an environment provides appropriate soil for the emergence and development of Ah Q's "spiritual victory method." The "spiritual victory method" was quite universal in that period, but its manifestation on the vagrant farmhand Ah Q has its particularities. This shows Ah Q under Lu Xun's pen is a highly individualized typical backward peasant deeply poisoned by feudal thoughts instead of an embodiment of abstract concepts. Second, detail descriptions are spectacular and vivid. For example, the lighting of lamps in the Zhao family is described in different paragraphs,

Kong Yiji, painted by Cheng Shifa

reflecting landlord Zhao's stingy personality in greater depths and making this character lifelike. Third, it has strong critical and satirical characteristics. Argumentative elements are interested into many parts of the novel. These humorous and incisive arguments give strong ideological and critical color to the work. Fourth, the novel contains accurate, clear, vivid and concise words with a strong sense of humor, and uses many ironies and exaggerations, showing Lu Xun's outstanding linguistic talent.

The True Story of Ah Q with its profound thoughts and great artistic achievements has become a classic among Chinese modern literary creations.

Ba Jin and His "Torrents Trilogy"

Ba Jin

Ba Jin (1904–2005), with the original name of Li Yaotang, was born in a big feudal family in Chengdu, Sichuan. In his literary career of more than 80 years, Ba Jin completed the "Torrents Trilogy" (*The Family*, *Spring* and *Autumn*), famous novels such as *A Garden of Repose* and *Cold Night* and prose works such as *Travel Notes*, *Confessions of Living* and *Random Thoughts*, and translated and introduced a lot of famous foreign works such as *Fathers and Sons* by Turgenev and *The Happy Prince by Wilde*.

Families are the society's cells, and in China's traditional patriarchal system, some special cultural meanings are attributed to "families." Ba Jin planned to write a novel to accuse old families' crimes and show his social ideals and life ideals in several years, and finally finished the "Torrents Trilogy" after a course of thinking and creation as long as ten years. *The Family* was written in 1931, *Spring* was written in 1938, and *Autumn* was completed in 1940. Because the original title of *The Family* is "Torrents," the three works are collectively called "Torrents Trilogy." The whole book with a length of more than one million Chinese characters established Ba Jin's important position in the history of Chinese modern literature.

Through describing the decline and split of the Gao family – a big feudal one, the "Torrents Trilogy" strongly accuses and attacks the crimes of the feudal patriarchal system and the old society with great anger and passion, exposes the decadence, degeneration, dissolution and shamelessness inside the dark feudal kingdom represented by the Gao family, and expresses the righteous call of those slaves at the bottom of the Gao family: "I want to be a man." The novel warmly eulogizes the increasing enlightenment and bold resistance of the Gao family's young generation represented by Gao Juehui, and reveals the historical development trend of the inevitable extermination of feudal families and the whole feudal social system through their break with the old family. Since *The Family* was published, more than 10 million copies have been sold! *In The History of Chinese New Literature*, the Hong Kong scholar Sima Changfeng praises *The Family* as "the most read novel in the history of new literature."

The most important artistic achievement of the "Torrents Trilogy" is that it successfully shapes various typical images in the big feudal family, among which the images of the three brothers in the Gao family (Juexin, Juemin and Juehui) are most representative. In particular, Juexin and Juihui have different personalities and destinies. They live under the same roof, but finally choose different lifestyles and ways of life. From them, people can see not only the common influence of the "family," but also the difference between their salient and unique personalities.

Juehui is a "childish but bold traitor." Many traits of Ba Jin himself can be seen from him. Juehui is the first person in the Gao family to accept new thoughts and the first person in the Gao

Various editions of *The Family*

In 1942, the famous dramatist Cao Yu adapted Ba Jin's novel *The Family* into a stage play, which became a never-failing classic drama on the stage of Chinese stage plays.

family to rise up in resistance. He dare ignore autocratic parents' authority and diametrically oppose "grandfathers in the Gao family." He actively participates in progressive students' movements, and openly supports his second elder brother Juemin to flee and resist arranged marriage. He opposes his eldest brother Juexin's "bow philosophy," sees his eldest brother obey his grandfather's will all the time, and scolds him as a "coward." He also breaks with the feudal family's idea of strict hierarchy, and boldly falls in love with the maid Mingfeng... At last, he cannot take it anymore, breaks with the suffocating family with great sadness and anger, devotes himself to the torrents of the times and society, and begins his new life.

Ba Jin showed not only the rebellious side of Juehui, but also the inherent weaknesses of Juehui as a young master in the feudal family. He is the Gao family's offspring after all. No matter how violently he resists, he unavoidably shows his inseparable ties with his family. Juehui's bold and rebellious character often contains immaturity and frailness, he is often impulsive rather than sensible, and he often overestimates the effect of individual resistance. Juehui under Ba Jin's pen is multi-faceted and complex. As a result, this image is lively and vivid.

Juexin is a "sacrifice buried with" the big feudal family. His archetype was Ba Jin's eldest brother. He is the most meaningful character with the most complex personality. Though Juexin is the Gao family's eldest young master, he is also influenced by the times and new thoughts, has

Still of TV series *The Family* adapted from Ba Jin's novel with the same title

his own pursuits and yearns for future life. He is emotional, sensitive and sympathetic, but he is a sick soul in great emotional distress under heavy pressure of feudal autocracy. Under the long-term influence of feudal ethical codes, Juexin appears extremely timid and forbearing. His own love is thoroughly ruined by his grandfather's words; he sympathizes with and understands the pursuit of his younger brothers and sisters and understands their dissatisfaction with the feudal family because he often has such dissatisfaction himself, but he becomes obsequious after his grandfather speaks; he often bumps into walls between feudal rulers and resisters very embarrassedly and painfully. In the eyes of both sides, he is an unprincipled, pathetic and useless person! He practices the "bow doctrine" throughout the big family, but in fact nobody is grateful to him. He consciously or unconsciously maintains the feudal family and feudal order. Readers also angrily denounce him sometimes, regarding him as an accomplice of feudal rulers!

The whole "Torrents Trilogy" analyzes a big family's prosperity and decline with its grand and meticulous artistic structure, and thus shows a cross-section of China's historical and cultural development. The work is full of enthusiasm and youthful energy, and has great momentum and strong tragic color. The "Torrents Trilogy" occupies an important position in the history of literature. More importantly, it has inspired several generations of Chinese people to think about the value of life and choose ways of life. It is both a literary classic and a classic about life.

Lao She and His Beijing Civil Society

Lao She (1899–1966), with the original name of Shu Qingchun, was a native of Beijing and a Manchu. He extensively practiced many artistic and literary styles, and his long novels and stage plays were most influential. His early works are long novels *The Philosophy of Old Zhang*, *Zhao Zi Says* and *Ma and Son* written during his teaching in Britain between 1924 and 1929 and revealing his unique artistic personality: he was good at depicting Beijing citizens' life humorously with broad vision. The period from his return to China in 1930 and the outbreak of the War of Resistance against Japan

Lao She

in 1937 is the second stage of Lao She's creation. During this period, he created long novels *The Tale of Cat City*, *Divorce and Rickshaw Boy*, medium-length novels *The Life of Niu Tianci* and *This Life of Mine*, short novel *Crescent Moon*, etc., sighed for the hardships of citizens at the bottom of the society, cried out against injustice, and built his unique Beijing citizens' society. After 1940s, Lao She's creation entered the stage of in-depth development. Representative works include long novels *The Drum Singers*, *Cremation* and *Four Generations under One Roof*, etc.

Lao She was very familiar with the social life of Beijing citizens at the bottom of the society. He tried to analyze the whole nation's inherent flaws from the perspective of the citizen class and expose the Chinese society's fundamental problems from the perspective of citizens.

Rickshaw Boy is Lao She's representative novel. He also deemed it as "my hit." The work tells the story of Xiangzi, a bankrupt young peasant who comes to Beiping and makes a living by pulling a rickshaw. He is hardworking, honest, kindhearted, righteous, ambitious, enterprising, responsible and sympathetic. His biggest wish is to buy a rickshaw and work for himself without being exploited by rickshaw owners. Though he works hard and fights tenaciously, setbacks come one after another: soldiers robs him of his first rickshaw bought with three years' savings; detective Sun relies on his power to extort the money saved by him through hard work to buy a rickshaw; after marrying Tiger Girl, he finally buys a rickshaw under her help, but Tiger Girl dies of dystocia, so he has to sell the rickshaw for funeral arrangements… At last, the cruel social reality not only crushes his dream, but also finally turns him into "a depraved, selfish and unlucky child born in the sick social environment and an ultimate victim of individualism."

Rickshaw Boy vividly reflects the sharp conflict between Xiangzi's life ideals and the social environment he is in, and truly reflects the chaos, darkness and decadence of the society and laboring people's miserable fate. The work describes the characteristics of Xiangzi such as a small producer such as selfishness, narrow-mindedness and overestimation of individual strength. The failure of his personal striving shows that under the social system of that period, laboring people could never "live well" on their own. The work depicts the endless pain and disaster brought to people in that era of tangled warfare among warlords, and shows the extreme poverty of laboring people at the bottom of the society. Under Lao She's pen, laborers living in Beiping's residential

An illustration in *Rickshaw Boy*, painted by Gu Bingxin

Still of TV series *Four Generations under One Roof* adapted from Lao She's novel with the same title

compounds occupied by many households lead inhuman miserable lives. Poverty changes their personalities. They beat their children, and scold their wives. Some of them even force their daughters to be prostitutes, and some cannot bear the humiliation and commit suicide… All these truly reflect the miserable life of people at the bottom of the society and shows Lao She's concern about citizens' fate.

Four Generations under One Roof is Lao She's longest work with a length of 800,000 Chinese characters, consisting of three parts: *Bewilderment*, *Ignominy*, and *Famine*. The work chooses

Lao She's works translated into foreign languages

Xiaoyangjuan Hutong, a very common alley in the west of Beiping as an epitome of this "fallen city" and unfolds a broad historical picture and a complicated plot centering on the circumstances of the four generations of the old-style businessman Qi Tianyou's family. It does not directly depict the all-out War of Resistance against Japan but analyzes the root causes of the nation's disaster in depth, showing the painful experiences of people in the enemy-occupied area in the War of Resistance against Japan and the course of their gradual awakening after disillusionment of the dream of momentary ease and their realization that sticking to the fight is the only way out. They are faithful and unyielding, fight hard, pay a hefty price, and finally win. The novel depicts the atrocity of Japanese invaders, the despicableness of various traitors, the kindheartedness, weakness and dejection of intellectuals, and the indomitable spirit of some citizens at the bottom of the society. *Four Generations under One Roof* with the pain of Beiping's citizens in the conquered country as theme makes up for the insufficiency of artistic and literary works reflecting citizens' life during the War of Resistance against Japan, and is a high monument in the course of Lao She's creation.

Apart from *Rickshaw Boy* and *Four Generations under One Roof*, stage play *Teahouse* created in 1957 is also one of Lao She's most influential works. *Teahouse* chooses Beijing's time-honored brand "Yutai Teahouse" as the specific scene where all sorts of people gather, and reflects the historical changes in the Chinese society and diversified and complicated human relationships and ways of the world in 50 years with the failure of the "Hundred Days' Reform" in 1898, the tangled warfare among warlords in the early period of the Republic of China and the Kuomintang's reactionary rule from the victory of the War of Resistance against Japan to the outbreak of the Liberation War as three cross-sections of time. *Teahouse* is Lao She's representative "Beijing-style" stage play with a strong cultural atmosphere of the "Beijing style." It has become an artistic treasure in the history of Chinese modern and contemporary stage plays and is reputed as "a miracle on the Eastern stage."

From *Rickshaw Boy* and *Four Generations under One Roof* to *Teahouse*, Lao She always focused on the civil society. The civil world is the main content and basic picture of his creations. Under Lao She's pen, Beijing people at the bottom of the society form a gallery of people with diversified but distinctive personalities. Lao She's works have strong local color of Beijing. The idiomatic expressions of the Beijing dialect and the indigenous customs of Beijing make his works reveal special national styles and thus exert important influence in China's literary circles. Lao She was always concerned about the issue of the national character reform, but his works have an honest, unsophisticated and humanistic flavor, full of understanding of and compassion for people at the bottom of the society. His works have distinctive humorous and satirical color but manifest love and tenderness. Lao She was good at writing stories, so his works all contain coherent and vivid plots and good stories, making Lao She's works easy to understand. As a result, Lao She was one of the modern writers most liked by readers.

Shen Congwen's World of West Hunan

Shen Congwen (1902–1988), with the original name of Shen Yuehuan, was born in Fenghuang County, Hunan. In his youth, he went to the borders of Hunan, Guizhou and Sichuan to learn about the social life, folkways and customs of Miao, Han and Tujia peoples. This became the life basis of his later literary creations, and formed his unique "rural" perspective of observation. Eulogizing and manifesting human nature was the consistent aesthetic ideal in Shen Congwen's creation. He idealized the "world of west Hunan" he was familiar with, eulogized its natural and simple folkways and manifested its harmonious and primitive beauty of human nature to resist the ugly social reality.

Shen Congwen

Border Town written in 1934 is Shen Congwen's representative work, describing the magnificent and cozy world of a "border town" and a paradise full of love and beauty. A love tragedy takes place in the border town. Ship owner Shunshun's eldest son Tianbao and second eldest son Nuosong both fall in love with an old boatman's granddaughter Cuicui, but Cuicui likes Nuosong. The old boatman only wants Cuicui to get happiness "independently," but he muddle-headedly causes Tianbao to propose through a matchmaker without knowing whom she loves after all. Tianbao's proposal is rejected. Feeling disappointed, he goes out by boat and gets drowned accidentally. After Tianbao's death, the old boatman knows Cuicui's thought, and acts as a go-between for Cuicui and Nuosong. He suddenly dies in depression in a stormy night after his failed attempt. After his eldest son dies, Shunshun does not approve Nuosong's request for marrying Cuicui at once. Nuosong leaves his hometown after a quarrel with his father. These "unfortunate coincidences" turn the love between Cuicui and Nuosong into a tragedy of "kindheartedness."

All characters in the story are ordinary and kindhearted people. The author seemed to write a tragedy in which "nobody does anything wrong" and only narrate the story consciously at the level of human nature without intending to explore the artificial, social and moral factors causing the tragedy. Through the unfolding, development and ending of the story, the work depicts and manifests everybody's "beautiful and natural life form consistent with human nature."

Border Town depicts two deeply moving images: Cuicui and the old boatman – her maternal grandfather.

Cuicui is an artistic image embodying the author's ideals of "love" and "beauty." Cuicui and his maternal grandfather depend on each other for survival in her childhood. Her "beauty" is gradually manifested through her love story. Her "love" is pure, natural and sincere, completely consistent with a young girl having just awakened to love. She is neither frivolous nor wild, showing her self-consciousness, self-complacence and self-respect for love. After falling in love with Nuosong, she does not expect Nuosong's elder brother Tianbao is also in love with her. Out of faith in and devotion to love, she turns Tianbao down, but as a result the love between Cuicui and Nuosong suffers a serious setback. Tianbao's death, Nuosong's departure from his hometown and her maternal grandfathers' sudden death make her "grow up" overnight. She feels painful and sad, but does not fall. She declines the ship owner's offer of letting her stay in his home, guards the ferry like her grandfather, waits for Nuosong's return, and fights against her twisted fate persistently with hope. Under Shen Congwen's pen, the scenery of the "border town" and Cuicui are integrated and "man and nature are united." She is a daughter of love, a daughter of nature and a fairy embodying beauty.

The old boatman embodies "kindheartedness." Having been ferrying travelers across the river for 50 years, he regards it as his bounden duty and willingly bears the burden of hard work. He is plain, honest, simple and chivalrous, not only refusing to accept travelers' money, but also treating villagers generously and kindly and thus winning villagers' respect. After the orphan is brought up, his biggest wish is to let Cuicui get love freely and happily. Therefore, he follows Miao people's marriage customs, lets Cuicui decide her marriage affairs and thinks the person who can sing "songs for three and a half years" and move her will be her husband. He knows he is too old, so he attends to this matter so urgently that he suddenly dies from depression. The author's depiction of the old boatman clearly shows an ordinary old man's broad mind full of human beauty and ethical beauty.

Border Town also has distinctive and unique characteristics in terms of artistic expression. The author combined depiction of characters' words and acts and depiction of psychologies to reveal characters' individual traits and abundant inner feelings. Particularly, while depicting Cuicui, the author observed quietly, conjectured the adolescent feelings and sexual psychologies manifested by the young girl sensitively, and highlighted Cuicui's shy, demure and tender personality vividly through rough external depiction and refined psychological depiction. The novel's structure is

Fenghuang Ancient Town. This is Shen Congwen's birthplace and the source of his inspiration in novel creation.

A woodcut created by Huang Yongyu for *Border Town*

Still of *film Border* Town adapted from Shen Congwen's novel with the same title

natural and smooth like floating clouds and flowing water. The whole novel gradually unfolds around the core of Cuicui's love story, making the plot focused and simple and at the same time perfectly combining the purity and complexity of the plot. The author also specially inserted descriptions of Miao people's customs of antiphonal singing, marriage proposal, provision of dowries, burial, etc. in the story's development, giving *Border Town* unique color of rural literature. Besides, *Border Town* also has a strong pastoral flavor. Cuicui's expectation of life is revealed at the end of the work: "This person might never come back and might come back 'tomorrow'!" The author could not have the heart to let Cuicui despair thoroughly, so he let her withstand tests and hardships for love and wait for her lover's return with hope. This leaves hopes, expectations and imaginations to readers, and gives the end a more lingering pastoral flavor.

The value of Shen Congwen's novel pursing perfect human nature to the history of Chinese modern literature is mainly manifested in two aspects: first, such persistent pursuit of perfect human nature is not only Shen Congwen's aesthetic ideal, but also his life ideal; second, such particular pursuit integrates perfect human nature with perfect society and perfect nature and constitutes the unique "world of west Hunan."

Eileen Chang's Life Legends

Eileen Chang

Eileen Chang (1921–1995), a native of Fengrun, Hebei born in Shanghai, became eminent and world-renowned almost overnight in Shanghai occupied by the enemy in 1940s. From 1943, her excellent works such as novel *Aloeswood Ashes* "The First Incense Brazier and the Second Incense Brazier," *Jasmine Tea*, *Love in a Fallen City* and *The Golden Cangue* emerged one after another. Later she published her novel collection *Legends* and her prose collection *Floating Words*.

Legends epitomizes the unique artistic style of Eileen Chang's literary creation: paying attention to absorbing artistic nutrition from Chinese traditional novels and meanwhile giving emphasis to drawing on the ideological methods and artistic skills of Western modern literature. The overall structure of *Legends* is like a traditional chapter-based novel, obviously influenced by Freud's psychoanalytic theory and integrating certain skills of Japanese new feeling novels into depiction of characters' feelings. Eileen Chang combined the advantages of refined literature and popular literature, pushed novels to the state of great elegance and popularity, and formed unique literary charm.

Eileen Chang was best at narrating "family history"

stories. Her generally recognized representative works include *Aloeswood Ashes: The First Incense Brazier*, *The Golden Cangue*, *Love in a Fallen City*, etc. *The Golden Cangue* deeply reveals the special magical relationship between money and life through the dual tragedies of the protagonist Cao Qiqiao's destruction by money and her destruction of others with money. The novel focuses on describing the protagonist Cao Qiqiao's life full of twists and turns and the course of her psychological perversion. Qiqiao is the daughter of a sesame oil shop's boss, ill-tempered and enchanting. After she marries into a rich family through her elder brother and sister-in-law, she suffers discrimination and marginalization greatly because of her humble family background. Her husband paralyzed since his childhood cannot satisfy her sexual desire, making her feel very painful. Though she gets a share of her husband's legacy after his death, long-term suppression of various kinds, suffering and influence of the old big family's atmosphere have thoroughly distorted her human nature. Her life is tightly shackled by gold. She only wants to accumulate wealth, has no familial feeling, even victimizes her daughter-in-law, ruins her daughter's marriage, constantly seeks sick release and retaliation against her family members, and becomes selfish, cruel, unreasonable and venomous in the course of crazy retaliation. The work demonstrates the course of destruction, devastation and extermination of Qiqiao's human nature in a multi-layered manner. She used to have a pretty young face, a longing for beautiful love and normal

Cover of [1944] No. 1 Issue of *Legends*

life pursuits, but she sacrifices all these for money. At the end of the novel, when she "feels the jade bracelet around her wrist and slowly pushes that bracelet upwards along her arm thin as a lath to her armpit, she cannot believe she had plump arms when she was young," and "when she looks back at her hard journey of 30 years, even the most beautiful moonlight seems a little bleak." The description of the dreary experiences of the character in the novel shows the author's deep hatred for and criticism of traditional feudal marriage, ethics and the world of money. The description of Cao Qiqiao in *The Golden Cangue* makes people feel shocked after shaking in fear and understand and sympathize with her more deeply after feeling disgusted.

Love in a Fallen City is another famous novel by Eileen Chang. The work tells the tragic fate of the female protagonist Bai Liusu born in a declining distinguished family. Though she and rich Chinese merchant Fan Liuyuan's marriage is realized dramatically and satisfactorily against the backdrop of war, the circumstances of her hard life including this accidentally completed marriage make Bai Liusu feel very sad and desolate. The "gray wall" in *Love in a Fallen City* shows the "desolate" background color of life more directly: "She was sure that the gray brick wall near Repulse Bay was still as strong and tall as ever. The wind stopped there, like three gray dragons coiling up on top of the wall, the moonlight glinting off their silver scales." This wall is mentioned three times in the novel, foreboding the "grey" keynote of life. Under Eileen Chang's pen, the bustling modern city suddenly collapses, and only this eternal "gray wall" is left. She used a lot of "gray" language to express this meaning. So when the human society's flashy appearance vanishes, all "gray things" are exposed nakedly to the public. In *Love in a Fallen City*, Eileen Chang also gave attention to using colors to depict characters and atmospheres, emphasized chromatic echoing between black and white colors and other colors, and thus showed the character's fate full of ups and downs. For example, depiction of Bai Liusu's psychology concisely manifests this artistic characteristic: she strikes a match, "the little three-cornered pennant of flaming red flickering in its own draft, coming closer and closer toward her fingers. With a puff of her lips, she blew it out, leaving only the glowing red flagpole. The pole twisted and shrank into a curly gray fiendish shape." A small match is gradually magnified into the focal image in the picture in the protagonist's vision from flaming red to gray and to a shape at last, showing Liusu feels embarrassed after being disdained, unwilling to yield and seeing no hope. This description is also a prediction of Bai Liusu's life and fate. After experiencing "flaming red" love, she finally realizes the goal of marriage. This is the best "red" burning period of her life like a burning match, but she fails to get love in the real

Still of TV series *Love in a Fallen City* adapted from Eileen Chang's novel with the same title

sense at last. After the war, her husband's original disposition is restored and his witty remarks only belong to other women. Therefore, after getting married, Liusu "is still a little bewildered" and becomes a "grey" shape in marriage like that burnt match with only her withered trunk left. Gray is always the background color throughout Eileen Chang's works. If red appears, it is only a small decoration in the middle. The past is gone forever, and recollecting the past "red" can only cause more disconsolation because the most splendid moment is also the saddest one.

Though she wrote legends full of changes, Eileen Chang living in turbulent times really yearned for stable things in normal society. Therefore, legendary stories actually still reveal the background color of common people's ordinary life. Just as she wrote on the title page of *Legends*, "The title of Legends is intended to look for ordinary people in legends and look for legends among ordinary people."

輕輕的我走了

正如我輕輕的来

我揮一揮衣袖

不帶走一片雲彩

——徐志摩《再別康橋》詩句

Modern Poetry: Looking for Its Own Voice

Around the May 4th Movement, Hu Shi's *Experimental Collection*, Guo Moruo's *The Goddesses*, Liu Bannong, Shen Yinmo, Liu Dabai, etc. shook the orthodox position occupied by old-style metrical poems for thousands of years with vernacular poetry, and created the new style of free vernacular new poetry. The Crescent Moon School of Poetry represented by Wen Yiduo and Xu Zhimo combined new poetry and metrics, pushing vernacular new poetry forward soon after its emergence. Around the 1930s, the Symbolic School of Poetry represented by Li Jinfa and the Modern School of Poetry represented by Dai Wangshu actively integrated the methods of Chinese and foreign poetry, and further opened space for modern new poetry's development. As a link between the preceding and the following, Ai Qing made important contributions to combining various schools' advantages and strengthening new poetry's free expansion. Mu Dan and the "Nine Leaves" poets blazed a new trail for Chinese modern poetry. In the liberated region, poems such as *Wang Gui and Li Xiangxiang* represented active efforts for nationalization and popularization. The poetry of 17 years is closely associated with the times and reality. A number of poets including Li Ji, Wen Jie, Guo Xiaochuan and He Jingzhi showed the new times and new life in many forms such as narrative poetry, lyric poetry, free poetry, metrical poetry, landscape poetry, historical and mythical poetry, love poetry and political satirical poetry.

Guo Moruo: Destruction and Creation

Guo Moruo (1892–1978), a native of Leshan, Sichuan, entered a private school in his childhood, went to Tokyo to study medicine in 1914, and later was obsessed with literature. Guo Moruo and students in Japan including Yu Dafu, Cheng Fangwu and Zhang Ziping established the Creation Society in 1921, and published the poetry collection *The Goddesses* in the same year. After the War of Resistance against Japan broke out in 1937, he returned to China and actively engaged himself in the movement of resisting Japan and saving the nation from extinction. Meanwhile, he also provided a wake-up call for the times and society with his literary creations, and put forward deep thoughts about the nation's fate. His historical dreams represented by Qu Yuan evoked great repercussions. "Unification of poetry and drama" is an important characteristic of all creations of Guo Moruo. His literary theories and creative practices with a special

In the photo of members of the Creation Society taken in 1926 are Wang Duqing, Guo Moruo, Yu Dafu and Cheng Fangwu (from left to right).

170

poetic quality show strong romantic characteristics, magical association and imagination, passionate creative spirit and creative talent.

The Goddesses is Guo Moruo's first collection of vernacular new poems and the first collection of new poems representing outstanding achievements and having huge influence in the history of Chinese modern literature. Though some new poetry collections emerged before the publication of *The Goddesses*, *The Goddesses* opened whole new space for Chinese modern poetry with brand new contents and forms. The emergence of *The Goddesses* let people see brand new consciousness of times, "a great resisting force" and a "manifestation of the 20th century's power" from Chinese poems and Chinese poets for the first time. *The Goddesses* deeply impressed readers in that period with its vigorous and magnificent style of poetry, grand and profound artistic conceptions and pure feelings not restricted by techniques. It can be said that the publication of *The Goddesses* ended the age of old poetry and at the same time started the age of new poetry.

Most poems in *The Goddesses* were written during the poet's overseas studies in Japan. *The Goddesses* clearly conveys the spirit of destroying the old, establishing the new, rushing forward and making giant strides during the "May 4th" Movement, and the surging imagination, rapid rhythms, grand momentum, magnificent colors and free style of poetry constitute its romantic characteristics. The "May 4th" Movement gave the poet intense emotions. His representative works such as *Nirvana of the Phoenix*, *The Heavenly Hound*, *Good Morning*, *Coal in the Stove* and *Goddess Regeneration* symbolically reflect the ancient nation's great awakening in the climax of the "May 4th" Movement from the commanding height of the times. Burning with bold denial and ruthless execration of all old order, old traditions and old ethical codes and calling for creation, brightness, democracy and progress like a tsunami, it excited and inspired a whole generation of people.

The unstrained genre of vernacular free poems with great momentum is the most peculiar and exciting creation in *The Goddesses*. They really opened new space for free poetry after the "May 4th" Movement. The emergence of these poems was, on the one hand, a manifestation of the poet's broad mind and abundant imagination and, on the other hand, a product of the spirit of the times surging during the "May 4th" Movement. Guo Moruo's free poetry breaks with traditional poetry's restrictions, having no fixed metric and form and even no end rhyme, but poems' internal melodies are harmonious and consistent with the poet's emotional beats. At many places, the poet

used overlapping and repeated lines to express endless imagination and emotion, arousing readers' strong inner excitement and making them angry, shout and resist with him. Just like his expectation in *Preface*, *The Goddesses* "pulled young people's heartstrings and enlightened them" during the "May 4th" Movement.

No other new poet ever achieved the momentum particular to *The Goddesses*. The words "good morning" shouted 27 times without a break are earthshaking, showing the poet's emotions, readers' resonance and the times' echoes and, more importantly, manifesting a creator's courage and air! As to that "heavenly hound" daring to swallow the universe and everything, people usually praise the poet's extraordinary imagination and exaggeration, but actually what is more important here is not imagination and exaggeration, but the poet's courage to imagine and exaggerate like that. Such courage enabled Guo Moruo's creations to always keep the general goal in sight at the height of history and times and directly have dialogues with times and history, with human society, with nature and with the whole universe. Therefore, Guo Moruo's poems have broad vision encompassing everything and supreme mighty power dominating everything.

In terms of poetry forms, Guo Moruo advocated "absolute freedom." He said, "I want to eliminate all poetry forms and write my own things with just the right flavor." *Nirvana of the Phoenix* is just a manifestation of his view. The form of poetic drama is adopted for the whole poem, the poem's atmosphere develops with the story harmoniously, the rhythm is clear and melodious, the sentence structures are variable, lively and free, not limited to one pattern and very suitable for singing and dancing.

Another glorious manifestation of Guo Moruo's "unification of poetry and drama" was his creation of historical dramas. *Qu Yuan* was written in 1942. Through Qu Yuan's tragedy, he manifested the major theme of opposing division and surrender, advocating unity in resisting foreign aggression, cursing darkness and eulogizing brightness with realistic significance, and expressed the Chinese nation's aspiration to strive for liberation in spite of violence. Guo Moruo's historical dramas represented by *Qu Yuan* formed a unique and salient artistic style and charm. In terms of material selection and cutting, it fully shows the association between history and reality, grasping history and opportunities of creation. *Qu Yuan* is based on the historical story of vertical integration for resisting the Qin State in the Warring States Period, which shares very similar spiritual connotations with the specific situation of China's War of Resistance against Japan in

Stage photo of Guo Moruo's historical drama *Tiger-shaped Tally*

the early 1940s; the protagonist Qu Yuan's personality and temperament also needed to be carried forward by the Chinese nation urgently in that period. In terms of reshaping of historical characters, Guo Moruo structured dramatic conflicts with characters' fates on the basis of depicting characters' personalities, revealed themes and pushed forward the drama's development through characters' powerful self-expression, and thus broke from modern stage plays' basic pattern of taking plot development as the main clue. Guo Moruo's creative elaboration and interpretation give a series of historical figures including Qu Yuan a realistic sense of nobility and greatness and a historical sense of profoundness and solemnity. Besides, Guo Moruo's historical dramas are often mingled with a lot of folk songs and lyric poems. Some appear repeatedly according to plot development, and some are chanted repeatedly by protagonists directly, such as *Ode to Tangerines* and *Ode to Thunder* and *Lightning in Qu Yuan, the poem on the journey* to the north in *Chinese Bush Cherry Flowers*, *Great Sadness* in *South Crown Grass*, the eulogistic song in *Tiger-shaped Tally*, etc. These lyric poems and songs not only strengthen the atmospheres, highlight the characters' personalities and enhance the script themes, but also integrate into the whole scripts as inseparable organic components. Guo Moruo was also good at using long soliloquies full of flavor in historical dramas to fully indicate characters' abundant and complicated inner feelings. Dialogues of characters in dramas and the author's narrations are also full of musical rhythms and poetic passion. Such poetic language shows the characteristic of unification of poetry and drama particular to Guo Moruo.

Xu Zhimo: Crescent Moon Poetry

The "Crescent Moon Society" was founded by Xu Zhimo and others in Beijing in 1923. In the early period, the main members included writers such as Hu Shi, Chen Yuan, Ling Shuhua and Lin Huiyin, professors and celebrities in various circles. In April 1926, Wen Yiduo and Xu Zhimo established the *Poetry* supplement of Beijing's *Morning Post*, began to clearly put forward theoretical views on modern new metrical poems, gathered a number of poets, and made active attempts to create new metrical poems. The new metrical poetry school was the early "Crescent Moon School of Poetry" marked by the establishment of the *Poetry* supplement. After 1928, Xu Zhimo founded the "Crescent Moon" bookstore in Shanghai with Hu Shi, etc., founded the Crescent Moon magazine with Liang Shiqiu, etc., gathered a number of young poets under the flag of the "*Crescent Moon*," and continued to actively explore new poetry. This was the later period of the "Crescent Moon School of Poetry." In both the early period and the later period, Xu Zhimo was

Photo of Xu Zhimo, Lin Huiyin and Thakur taken during Indian poet Thakur's visit to China in 1924

a representative figure in it and could be called the soul of the "Crescent Moon School of Poetry."

The "Crescent Moon School of Poetry" systematically elaborated the theory of new poetry's metrics, and emphasized that the most important aesthetic features of new poetry should be "harmony" and "regularity," most prominently manifested in Wen Yiduo's proposal on poetry's "three beauties" (i.e. "architectural beauty, musical beauty and pictorial beauty"). The new metrical poetry school's "newness" lay in elimination of various rules of classical Chinese, old rhymes and old-style metrical poetry, emphasis on syllables and rhythms in poems, inheritance of the essence of classical poetry and innovation, represented by Xu Zhimo's poems. The "Crescent Moon School of Poetry" also advocated nature, gave attention to "personalities," translated a lot of foreign poems, transplanted a lot of foreign poetry styles and forms, and injected new emotional vitality and expression ability into the development of Chinese modern new poetry.

Xu Zhimo (1897–1931), a native of Haining, Zhejiang, studied in the University of Shanghai, Peiyang University in Tianjin and Peking University. He went to the United States for overseas studies in 1918 and transferred to the University of Cambridge in Britain to work on political economy in 1920, but he was more interested in modern British aesthetic poetry and began to create poems at the same time. He returned to China in 1922, and continued to engage in poetry creation while teaching at a university. In November 1931, he died in a plane crash. Xu Zhimo's main works include *Zhimo's Poems* (1925), *A Night in Florence* (1927), *Tiger* (1931) and *Roaming* (1932). Besides, he also created nearly 100 uncollected poems and translated poems.

As the representative poet of the Crescent Moon School, Xu Zhimo tried to make achievements in metrics. He thought that new poetry should create perfect metrics. In the practice of poetry creation, he created diversified genres and styles of poetry. In his first poetry collection *Zhimo's Poems*, the relationship between lines and stanzas is handled in different ways. There are three-line stanzas, eight-line stanzas and ten-line stanzas, and some poems have no stanzas. He used various formats to create new poetry, and brought about a new trend of new poetry. He mostly adopted Western poetry's rhymes. For example, he used the AABB rhyme pattern for *Sir! Sir!*, the AABB rhyme pattern for *To Look for a Star* and the ABAB rhyme pattern for *He's Afraid to Open his Mouth*, revealing change in harmonious rhymes in poetry.

Xu Zhimo paid attention to poems' overall beauty. He deemed a poem as an organic whole,

giving emphasis to association and proportion between the parts and the whole. This is Xu Zhimo's specific view on poetry aesthetics under the guidance of the overall aesthetic principle of perfect forms. To attain the state of poems' overall beauty, he often used symmetrical and overlapping sentences. Take *Saying Good-bye to Cambridge Again*, for example. There were many famous scenic spots near Cambridge, but the poet focused on depicting the River Cam and used the method of repetition at the beginning or end of each stanza. The ABCB rhyme pattern is adopted for each four-line stanza, and the melody is harmonious and full of musical beauty. In the first short four-line stanza, the word "quietly" appears three times, creating a lively rhythm in sentiment and making the whole poem immersed in the beauty of repetitive rhythms and rhymes.

The greatest influence of Xu Zhimo's creation on new poetry was the musicality of his poems. He was the best practitioner of "musical beauty" advocated by the Crescent Moon School. He thought that just like blood circulation was the secret of every person's body, a poem's secret was the regularity and flow of the syllables in it. Therefore, Xu Zhimo meticulously organized every poem's rhymes and metrics. He wrote in *A Snowflake's Happiness*, "If I were a snowflake, drifting

The magazine *Crescent Moon* published in March, 1928

suavely in mid-air, I would recognize my direction – soaring, soaring, soaring – The ground below holds my direction." There are three pauses in each line of the poem, and each pause consists of two to four Chinese characters, forming a slow rhythm. The "-ake" and "-air" rhymes are open and soft, corresponding to the charm of drifting snowflakes. The tune and rhyme are changed from the third sentence, and the more sonorant and rising "-ion" and "-ing" rhymes are used. The whole poem with harmonious rhymes is graceful and smooth, having a kind of natural beauty. In poems such as *Roaming, Saying Good-bye to Cambridge Again* and *I Bought a Handful of Lotus Seed Pods beside the Yangtze River*, musicality emerges from interaction between rhymes and feelings, realizing integration of "spiritual music" and "rhetorical music."

Besides, Xu Zhimo's poems are spiritually transcendental, natural, beautiful and highly individualized. For example, though the famous poem Sayonara consists of only five lines, it vividly depicts the bearing, feelings and psychological activities of the "Japanese girl" at the time of saying goodbye to her friend. It is graceful, soft and peaceful, with expectation in sorrow. The whole poem is permeated with a complex emotion and can be called the best poem of the New Crescent School.

Hu Shi made such a summary for Xu Zhimo, "His view on life is really a pure belief in three words: love, freedom and beauty." Zhu Ziqing praised Xu Zhimo's poems, saying "they are a river of life gurgling day and night." If Guo Moruo let people see new poems could be written this way, then Xu Zhimo let people see new poems written this way were great!

Ai Qing: A Modern Poem Rooted in Earth

Ai Qing

In the course of Chinese modern new poetry's development, Ai Qing was a poet linking the preceding and the following. He fully absorbed the liveliness and freedom of vernacular new poetry since the May 4th Movement, created the unique framework of prose beauty featuring inner precision and harmony, and made positive contributions to modern new poetry's constant development.

Ai Qing (1910–1996), a native of Jinhua, Zhejiang Province, was born in a landlord family but was breast-fed by a poor countrywoman. This special life experience exerted profound and major influence on the formation of Ai Qing's personality and his later poetry creation. Ai Qing liked fine arts in his childhood, studied painting at the National West Lake Academy of Art in Hangzhou at first, and then went to France under a work-study program. In Paris, French and European impressionistic paintings, especially the works of later impressionist masters such as van Gogh characterized by intense display of colors and creative expression of subjective feelings, not only influenced Ai Qing's painting, but also influenced his later poetry creation. While studying in France, Ai Qing extensively read many Western poets' works. Verhaeren was among the poets who influenced Ai Qing the most.

Ai Qing returned to China in early 1932, and was arrested and put into prison for joining the Left Wing Artist Association and participating in progressive activities in Shanghai. Ai Qing began to write poems in prison. After being released from prison, Ai Qing published his first poetry collection *Dayanhe* at his own expenses. Ai Qing's most influential representative work *Dayanhe – My Wet-Nurse* in it established his fame. This is an autobiographical lyric poem with the poet's childhood nurse Dayanhe as the protagonist, eulogizing Dayanhe's excellent character of steadfastness, tolerance, plainness and kindheartedness with infinite compassion and deep love, depicting her life of poverty and humiliation, and powerfully cursing the old world full of crime. Dayanhe is a precious artistic model of Chinese countrywomen depicted in new poems, and her fate was the common tragic fate of all oppressed countrywomen in China. Ai Qing associated Dayanhe's fate with the fates of innumerable people like her: "Dedicated to all of them on earth, the wet-nurses like my Dayanhe, and all their sons."

Dayanhe – My Wet-Nurse is an unrhymed free-style poem written in pure spoken language without artificially arranged rhymes, moving people with candid and sincere feelings. However, Ai Qing paid attention to use of parallelism and repetition, formed a rhythm of emotional change, gave the poem a strong melody and sense of rhythm, and achieved the artistic effect of soul-stirring and lingering charm.

Around the outbreak of the War of Resistance against Japan, Ai Qing actively engaged in the movement of saving the nation from extinction and created nearly 100 poems in several years. Perhaps because Ai Qing was influenced by Van Gogh, many of his poems eulogize the sun. *The Sun* is the most representative one among them, showing the poet's conviction in the forthcoming revitalization of the nation and human happiness bound to be achieved. *The Sun* with great passion, firm faith and unrestrained spirit gives overwhelming, thunderous and powerful momentum to the sun, and truly expresses the "voice of the times:" the great revitalization of the Chinese nation.

However, Ai Qing was not a blindly optimistic poet. His joy and firmness coexisted with grief, indignation and melancholy. In the War of Resistance against Japan, he travelled to most parts of the country, saw the cruel reality of war, witnessed the misery of destitute and homeless Chinese laboring people in war, and felt the nation was at the verge of extinction. The works written in this period including *The Woman Mending Clothes*, *Beggar* and *Wheelbarrow* mostly have strong melancholy color.

Ai Qing consciously pursued prose-style poetry, specially emphasized new poetry's "prose beauty," opposed those flowery words and sentence structures, and thought prose-style language should be used to capture real poems in life. Ai Qing's poems are also highly impressionistic thanks to his great accomplishments in fine arts. He was good at using colors, exaggerating lights as well as picture and line arrangements to enhance images' distinctiveness. Though the images depicted by him were from real life, he often used novel metaphors and abundant imaginations to make the images generated by him more appropriate than real life. *Wheelbarrow* is an example of perfect integration of scenes, feelings, lights, colors, pictures and even sounds in Ai Qing's poetry:

In the territory where the Yellow River once flowed,
In numberless dried-up riverbeds,
The wheelbarrow,
With its single wheel,
Lets out a squeal that shakes the lugubrious sky,
Piercing the wintry chill, the desolate stillness.
From the foot of this mountain
To the foot of that mountain,
The sound cuts right through
The sorrow of the northern people.

On frost-bitten, snow-chilled days,
In and around destitute little villages,
The wheelbarrow,
With its solitary wheel,
Carves out its deep ruts in the pale-yellow layers of earth,
Cutting through the vastness and the desolation,
From this road
To that road,
It knits together
The sorrow of the northern people.

Ai Qing's poems can never be separated from land, which supports all his poems like faith. Therefore, Ai Qing is reputed as "Land Poet." *I Love This Land* written in 1938 clearly reveals the poet's deep and warm feeling toward the motherland:

If I were a bird,
I would sing with my hoarse voice
Of this land buffeted by storms,
Of this river turbulent with our grief,
Of these angry winds ceaselessly blowing,
And of the dawn, infinitely gentle over the woods…
– Then I would die
And even my feathers would rot in the soil.
Why are my eyes always brimming with tears?
Because I love this land so deeply…

Ai Qing's promotion of modern new poetry was manifested in two aspects: first, in terms of poems' emotional connotations, Ai Qing was always concerned about the nation's future and fate in writing poems and at the same time extended his vision to the whole humanity's future and fate, showing the poet's broad mind; second, in terms of poems' artistic forms, Ai Qing fully absorbed various accomplishments of world poetry in writing poems and at the same time always kept artistic expressions deeply rooted in his nation's soil. He used the "reed flute brought back from Europe" to play music with strong national flavor.

Mu Dan: Abundance and the Pain of Abundance

Mu Dan

Mu Dan (1918–1977), a native of Haining, Zhejiang, was both a poet and a top Chinese translator. He was admitted to the Department of Foreign Languages of Tsinghua University in 1935, fled to the south after the outbreak of the War of Resistance against Japan, and taught at National Southwestern Associated University formed by Peking University, Tsinghua University and Nankai University. At National Southwestern Associated University, Mu Dan was fully influenced by Western modern poetry, enthusiastically translated and introduced works of Western modern poets such as Eliot, Rilke and Auden, and actively discussed new poetry's development and poetry theories.

The poetry collections *Expedition, Collected Poems by Mu Dan* and *Flag* published by Mu Dan in 1940s became important achievements in China's poetry circles in that period. The works created by Mu Dan in this period are solemn and serious, fully expressing strong doubt about traditions and order and rebellious spirit in the pursuit of integration of sensibility and sense. He hurriedly jumped into the vortex of the times, showed the conflict and struggle between the soul and body, and clearly demonstrated the qualitative difference between his poetry and traditional poetry. In *The Besieged*, he fully expressed the spirit of rebellion against traditions, "A circle: the work of so many years, Our despair will make it complete. Destroy it, friends! Let us ourselves Be a gap in it: worse than mediocrity. Then lightning and rain, new temperature and hope Can pour in, topple reverence. For we are besieged multitude, Only when we stir can the new land awaken." In his view, the traditions with the "circle" as the model were just "mediocrity" completed by "our despair," and though incompleteness meant destruction, danger and even sacrifice, it would bring the hope of new life. Such "siege-breaking" consciousness was not only an artistic thought, but also a modern attitude towards life and realistic spirit, closely associated with a series of changes including the poet's poetic spirit and life experience.

Violence is the core of Mu Dan's poems full of eternal violent binary opposition: sense and desire, gods and demons, pain and hope, exile and permanent homes… "From compulsive collective foolishness to civilization's meticulous calculation, from the overthrow of our life values to their establishment and reestablishment: we still trust your iron fist the most. From our present nightmare to tomorrow's paradise hard to come by, from a baby's first cry to his unwilling death: everything is inherited from your image." (*Violence*) But for Mu Dan, violence was not only devastation of human nature, but also a test of human nature. Therefore, he automatically abandoned the emotional parts of traditional poetry, experienced the cruel reality of relationships between different people and between people and society through serious reflection, perceived human nature from a rational perspective, revealed people's absurdity and despair, and sublimated a specific hardship in real life into an abstract philosophical thought. In self-analysis, he felt an anxiety of life: "After coming out from the womb, I lost warmth. The missing part longed for help. I am always myself, isolated in the wilderness, Separated from the group in a still dream, Feeling the stream of time painfully, grasping nothing, And reminiscing constantly, but I cannot bring myself back." (*Self*) The "self" is isolated in time and space, cannot integrate into the whole history and group, cannot seize and grasp anything, and has lost overall harmony and become an "incomplete self." Here the "self" is not Mu Ji himself. Instead, it has sublimated into man's general individual existence. In *Spring*, Mu Dan expressed passionate adolescent desire like "green flames flickering upon the grass," but such desire of life to embrace spring is curled and prohibited and finds no home: "Under the blue sky, obsessed by an eternal enigma is Our tightly-closed body of 20-year-old, Just like birdsongs earth-cast. You are kindled, curled, but find no home. O light, shade, sound, color, all now naked, And in pain, waiting to enter into new combinations." The manifestation of

oppression of such desire of life in Mu Dan's poems comes from not only "historical conflict," but also invisible inhibition of individual rationality.

However, Mu Dan's thought does not lead to decadence and despair. His poems reveal a kind of unrest consciousness of life and stubborn spirit in the soul's struggle: "Stay alive on the dangerous land. Live in the dying group, When all phantoms turn hideous and all strengths are like exposed seas, cruel, devastative and ferocious, Just like you and I gradually get strong but die, that immortal person." The significance of life is struggle in the life of "hope, disillusionment, hope and the will to live on" (*Stay Alive*).

Mu Dan's poems are deeply rooted in his times. On the one hand, he was greatly oppressed by reality, and on the other hand, he boldly intervened into and embraced reality with the consciousness of an upright intellectual and a sense of social responsibility. He cried excitedly in the poem *Glorification*:

I will, with the desolate desert, bumpy roads, and mule-drawn cart,
I will, with a trough boat, a mountain of wild flowers, and overcast and rainy weather,
I will embrace you with all, you,
The people I see everywhere, O,
People living in humiliation, stooping people,
I will embrace you one by one with my blood-stained hands,
Because a nation has stood up.

In 1942, Mu Dan burning with patriotic fervor joined the Chinese Expedition Force, fought on the battleground of Burma in the War of Resistance against Japan, and experienced all kinds of hardships in the Battle of the Wild Man Mountain that shocked the whole world. So he wrote *Enchantment of the Forest – Offering Sacrifices to the White Bones in the Hukawng River* to commemorate his comrades-in-arms who died in this battle. It is full of the poet's philosophical thoughts on man's situation and way out in the 20th century marked by incessant war and dispute and is a representative work directly addressing war and death and eulogizing life and eternity in the history of Chinese modern poetry. *Glint* can be called the best epic created by Mu Dan in terms of either the poem's connotations or the poem's form. *In Glint*, Mu Dan focused on seeking to solve the issue of modern people's puzzles about their situation from the perspective of metaphysics. He saw that the nation was suffering and that people would lose themselves on the verge of spiritual collapse. This urged him to proceed from the specific times and region he lived in, rise to broader space and time, understand internal life and structural grandeur at a higher level and seek to realize a new world full of hope for people's spirit. He arduously explored paths to a new world in many aspects such as nature, society and life. Deep emotions run through *Glint* featuring grand structures, solemn sentence patterns and overwhelming vigor and momentum. This epic thought, in a certain sense, marked the depth of Chinese modern poets' metaphysical thinking about this war that deeply influenced the whole humanity, and marked Chinese modern poetry's expansion to the depths of reality and history as well as the essence of individual life.

Mu Dan's poems are full of abundant life experience, containing painful thoughts about diversified life.

Modern Stage Plays: Transplantation and Development

Stage plays were transplanted from foreign countries to China. Back in 1906, the Spring Willow Society formed by Chinese students in Japan began to explore this new literary genre of stage plays, but what really laid a foundation for modern stage plays were *Thunderstorm* and *Sunrise* written by Cao Yu in the mid-1930s. Besides, Xia Yan's *Under the Eaves of Shanghai*, Tian Han's *Death of a Noted Actor*, etc. jointly contributed to the prosperity of modern stage play creation. After the founding of the People's Republic of China in 1949, active efforts were made for stage plays, opera, traditional Chinese opera, adaptation of traditional dramas, etc. Among them, Lao She's *Teahouse*, Tian Han's *Guan Han Qing*, Guo Moruo's *Cai Wenji* and Cao Yu's *Courage and the Sword* are representative works. Since the 1980s, a number of playwrights have explored bravely and formed the trend of diversified stage play creations. For example, *Magic Cube*, *Death Visits the Living*, etc. explore different philosophical meanings of life in depth. At the turn of the century, stage plays such as *No. 1 Tower in the World*, *Xiaojing Lane*, *Neighbors* and *Wangfujing* continued to give attention to social development and the fate of people at the bottom of the society, and became classic new stage plays.

Cao Yu: Born for Drama

Cao Yu

Cao Yu (1910–1996), with the original name of Wan Jiabao, was born in an old-style bureaucratic family, and witnessed many "messy people and things" as a result. Perhaps because of his family, he was deeply influenced by Chinese and foreign drama in his childhood and laid a foundation for later stage play creation. In the autumn of 1922, Cao Yu passed the entrance examination of the new-style Nankai high school, became a member of the "Nankai New Dramas Society," and performed Ibsen's *An Enemy of the People* and *Nala* and Molière's *The Miser*. This was a good opportunity to develop his interest in literature and drama fostered in his childhood. Cao Yu passed the entrance examination of Nankai University's Department of Political Science in 1928, transferred to Tsinghua University in 1930, and worked on Western literature. In this period, he read a lot of dramas by the three Greek tragedy writers, Molière, Ibsen, O'Neill and Chekhov. Systematic studied significantly improved Cao Yu's drama theory.

In 1933, while studying at Tsinghua University, Cao Yu completed his first stage play *Thunderstorm*, which was published on *The Literature Quarterly* upon Ba Jin's recommendation, publicly performed for the first time in

1935, and was warmly welcomed by the audience. At present, Thunderstorm is still a never-failing Chinese stage play. Cao Yu later created *Sunrise* (1936), The *Wilderness* (1937) and *Peking Man* (1940), and adapted Ba Jin's famous novel *The Family* into a stage play in 1942. These works showed Cao Yu's continuous exploration of stage play art, marked maturity of Chinese stage play creation, and at the same time established Cao Yu's place in the history of Chinese modern stage plays.

Thunderstorm is Cao Yu's first work that made him famous. The author wrote the work at the age of 23, fully showing his outstanding artistic talent. Actually, Cao Yu planned to create *Thunderstorm* after graduating from senior high school. After five years' repeated contemplation and revision, he finally completed the work before graduating from college and made that soul-stirring "first groan or cry" to people in the world.

In view of the theme of *Thunderstorm*, it was really influenced by some Western drama traditions, especially the American writer Eugene O'Neill, mainly depicting a big upper-class family's incestuous relationships and a series of life tragedies caused as a result, but the author went far beyond the scope of this theme itself in terms of exploration of ideological connotations and pursuit of artistic expression. The drama not only reflects the social system's irrationality revealed by the big family's destruction and the trend of its inevitable collapse. More importantly, while showing the family tragedy and the social tragedy, the drama also depicts a more complex and profound fate tragedy: the irreconcilable huge contradiction between people's fight against fates and fates' domination of people. As Cao Yu wrote in *Preface to Thunderstorm*, he always had an "indescribable longing for many mysterious things in the universe."

Zhou Puyuan is the protagonist in the whole drama. This character's connotations and charisma lie in his character and fate full of profound contradictions. Zhou Puyuan goes to Germany for overseas studies in his early years, comes into contact with the capitalist social trends of freedom and democracy to some extent, and falls in love with Shiping, a young maid in his family, under the influence of the thought of pursuing freedom, individuality and true love. However, he finally yields under pressure from the feudal consciousness of traditions and the feudal concept of families, abandons Shiping and their son born three days ago, and marries Fanyi, a rich and influential family's daughter. Here, Zhou Puyuan not only abandons Shiping and her son, but also denies the thought of freedom and sincere emotion pursued by him in his early years as well as his conscience.

However, this choice of his also has a certain involuntary factor. From the beginning of that tragedy, Zhou Puyuan is in a painful dilemma: he ruthlessly destroys Shiping and causes a cruel tragedy, but he is also a victim in this tragedy because selling the soul is always an indescribable mental torment for him. Thus Zhou Puyuan becomes an extremely selfish, cruel and hypocritical person. The face of a hypocritical philanthropist, the authority of a cruel feudal parent and his inner selfishness and darkness make Zhou Puyuan's character quite complex. Particularly, his attitude towards Shiping fully reveals his innermost contradictions and complex feelings: ZhouP Puyuan is deeply guilty of the forced "death" of Shiping; he always remembers Shiping's birthday and arranges the house in the style liked by Shiping "before death." This feeling with a certain sense of confession is not hypocritical, but Shiping's "death" is the precondition of this true feeling. So when Shiping appears in front of him alive unexpectedly, his selfish, cruel and hypocritical nature comes back again. He angrily scolds Shiping upon her arrival, tries to wash away his sins with money, and turns Shiping away mercilessly again. It should be seen that facing Shiping's appearance, Zhou Puyuan not only directly feels a realistic threat to his status, fame and interests, but also subconsciously feels a predestined blow of his fate! This makes him more fearful. Actually in the course of destroying the whole family, Zhou Puyuan also destroys himself, and while causing a tragedy to others, he is also mercilessly punished by the fate. This is the more profound meaning of *Thunderstorm*.

Fanyi is another core character in *Thunderstorm*. In view of her fate, she is first of all a victim. She used to be influenced by new thoughts, pursue independent personality, aspire to beautiful life and be full of life passion, but fate throws her into the "cruel well" of the Zhou family, torments her and gradually turns her into a "stone-like person." She not only fails to get love, but also fails to get basic human freedom and dignity. Cao Yu fully understood and sympathized with her, attributing the most "thunderous" resistant personality to her. She hates Zhou Puyuan's ruthlessness and the unfair fate, struggles without any support in the Zhou family, and painfully burns her life. Her resistance against Zhou Puyuan's feudal tyranny and oppression of human nature is of typical epoch-marking significance, but her personality and resistance are also full of contradictions and perplexities. As a "cornered beast," she falls in love with Zhou Ping regardless of human relations. Such "love" is so abnormal and perverted, but Fanyi clings to it firmly. She despises Zhou Ping's selfishness, hypocrisy and cowardice, but such "love" has become the most meaningful thing in her life: This is not only a manifestation of the value of her existence and a crazy retaliation against Zhou Puyuan, but also the only effective struggle against fate. Such struggle mingled with extremist

Stage photo of stage play *Thunderstorm*

individualism and the social significance of the times makes Fanyi's personality and destiny reveal a dual mental tragedy. Her "love" and hate mingle numerous contradictions at different levels including the contradiction between individuals and the society, the contradiction between self-respect and morality and the contradiction between oneself and others. Her loneliness and pain are potential dynamites in the Zhou family, her existence makes all people related to the Zhou family including Zhou Puyuan feel suppressed and fearful, and she finally becomes the "detonator" for the Zhou family's various tragic clues. Zhou Puyuan ruins others and buries himself; Fanyi burns herself and also ruins others. The difference is that Fanyi's self-burning contains elements deserving sympathy, while her destruction of others is more mentally shocking and astounding.

Cao Yu's dramas are most characteristic of the Chinese nation. He successfully showed China's social life and the fates of Chinese characters with foreign artistic forms, and ingeniously mingled them with Chinese artistic expression modes; Cao Yu was best at absorbing foreign artistic accomplishments into his dramas, skillfully used foreign drama theories and techniques of performing drama on the stage, and amazed Chinese readers and audiences with new artistic forms of stage plays. Cao Yu's active exploration in these two aspects truly laid a foundation for the maturation of Chinese modern stage plays.

Tian Han: Drama like Life

Tian Han

Tian Han (1898–1968) was a native of Changsha, Hunan. His father died in his childhood, and her family was poor. He passed the entrance examination of Changsha Normal College to become a state-funded student in 1912, and went to Japan to pursue studies after his graduation in 1916. He studied the navy at first and education afterwards, but he deeply loved literature and drama. While studying in Japan, he joined the Chinese Teenagers' Society and began to publish papers on literature and art and one-act plays. As one of the founders of the Creation Society, Tian Han held very distinctive and peculiar opinions on romantic literature. He returned to China in 1922, actively engaged in drama activities, and founded the "Southern China Society" and "Southern China Art Academy" in the mid-1920s. After the outbreak of the War of Resistance against Japan, he actively organized drama performance teams and publicity teams for resisting enemies, and ran around for resistance through literature and art. After the founding of the People's Republic of China, he served as Chairman of the China Theatre Association, Vice Chairman of the China Federation of Literary and Art Circles, etc. Tian Han created, adapted and translated dozens of stage play, drama and film scripts, and wrote a lot of poems, prose and comments. The lyrics of the national anthem of the People's

Republic of China *March of the Volunteers* were written by him.

Tian Han's creations are roughly divided into two stages with 1930 as the dividing point. His early scripts such as *A Night in the Coffee Shop* and *A Night of Capturing the Tiger* mostly have the theme of opposing feudal tyranny and demanding freedom of marriage and reflect the petite bourgeoisie's wish and demand for personality emancipation. His scripts have an aesthetic tendency and reveal strong sentimental and melancholy feelings. I the period from Tian Han's assumption of the office of the President of Shanghai Art University in 1927 to the establishment of the "League of Leftist Writers" in 1930, Tian Han's thought changed and created many stage plays represented by *Death of a Noted Actor*, *Scenery of a Riverside Village*, *Night Talk of Suzhou*, *A Tragedy of the Lake* and *Return to the South*. One type is social dramas directly exposing the dark side of reality, and the other type is symbolic plays with metaphoric implications. Social dramas such as *Death of a Noted Actor* reflect the gradual inclination of Tian Han as a romantic-lyric-poet-like playwright towards realism and manifest his will to expose the dark side of life through artistic creation. Symbolic dramas such as *Return to the South* show organic combination of Tian Han's romantic feelings and symbolic expression methods, and manifest his will to make life artistic, beautiful and poetic.

In the spring of 1930, Tian Han participated in the leftist literature and art movement and was elected Chairman of the League of Chinese Left-Wing Dramatists. His creation matured in the period from 1930 to 1937. He wrote about 20 dramas including *Plum Rains*, *1932 Moonlight Melody*, *Disorderly Bell Sounds*, *Before Dawn*, *Flood* and *Spring Melody*. Their common features are: drawing on the reality, reflecting sharp ethnic conflicts and chaos in domestic social life, flowing with elated artistic spirit, and winning with passion and momentum. From the outbreak of the War of Resistance against Japan in 1937 to 1949, Tian Han not only created stage plays with the theme of the war of resistance, but also extensively united old dramatists to save the nation, wrote new traditional Chinese dramas for them, created *New Heroes and Heroines*, a large-scale historical opera depicting the story of the heroes who defeated Japan in the Ming Dynasty, actively participated in the activities of progressive film circles, and created film script *Recalling the South of the Yangtze River*, etc. After 1949, he created famous dramas such as *Guan Hanqing*.

Tian Han was one of the pioneers of Chinese modern stage plays. The artistic style of his stage plays was mainly manifested in the following aspects. First, he was good at shaping artistic

Stage photo of stage play *Death of a Noted Actor*

images and, in particular, displaying characters' ideological personalities and tragic fates from the dual perspective of life and drama. The three-act stage play *Death of a Noted Actor* completed in 1929 is a typical Tian Han-style society-plus-art drama. The work tells the tragic story of the famous elderly male character actor Liu Zhensheng's death on the stage, shows Tian Han's deep understanding and comprehension of society, life and art, and focuses on revealing the tragic fates of actors in the dark society emphasizing money instead of art. The significance of this image not only lies in description of the tragic fates of artists looked down upon in that period. More importantly, the author discovered their valuable spirit of clinging to art and dedicating themselves to art. Liu Zhensheng "attached most importance to drama morals and drama flavors." He did not take art as material capital for pursing enjoyment in life but did everything possible to maintain the artistic spirit of truth, goodness and beauty in the decadent atmosphere of commercial drama. In his opinion, "that thing (Beijing opera) is more important than life." Therefore, he felt extremely sad when seeing his female disciple Liu Fengxian's fall and died tragically.

Second, his works have strong legendary and story-telling color. Tian Han was always rooted in real life, proceeding from contradictions in life and trying to combine necessity, chance, romance and reality. This not only enhances his dramas' artistic effect, but also is conducive to depicting characters' personalities and expressing core themes. For example, the plot of *Spring Melody* has strong romantic legendary color. *Death of a Noted Actor* further integrates the stage of art and the stage of life naturally and ingeniously, forming the unique drama-in-drama effect of actors playing actors, showing the broad typical social environment in the limited space and time on the drama stage and having strong artistic expression ability and appeal. The work adopts the structure of parallel development different from the single structure of Tian Han's early works. The two basic clues mingled with several other clues make the simple script structure complex and show various characters' different personalities

Third, his language is highly emotional. Tian Han engaged in stage play creation as a lyric poet. He was good at drawing on Western stage plays' expression methods, absorbed traditional Chinese opera's characteristics, and tried to explore Chinese stage plays' national style. He used poetry and music as means of expressing emotions, making dramas emotionally and musically beautiful. He experienced life very subjectively, attached importance to expressing characters' inner emotions, depicting the ideal state and pursing poetic artistic conceptions, and created a highly emotional atmosphere.

New Period – New Trends of Poetry

Poems created in the new period directly face life, reflect on history, change the reality and reveal the truth of life. Poets, especially young poets, under the dual influence of Western modernism and Eastern classical poetry, reflected and manifested the world with their special aesthetic feelings, aesthetic evaluations and pursuit of ideals. The rise of poets of the obscure school including Shu Ting, Gu Cheng and Bei Dao among them was especially prominent. At the turn of the century, pioneering and exploratory poetry received a lot of attention. Representative poets such as Hai Zi, Ouyang Jianghe, Xi Chuan, Wang Jiaxin, Yi Sha and Zhai Yongming came either from among the people or from schools, but their persistent exploration of poetry forms injected new vitality into Chinese new poetry's continuous development.

The Rise of "Obscure Poetry"

In 1978, the literary magazine *Today* founded by Bei Dao and Mang Ke brought about an upsurge of obscure poetry.

The rise of "obscure poetry" was one of the most important events in the poetry movement of the new period. At the end of the 1970s, China ended the turmoil of the "Cultural Revolution" and began to implement the policy of reform and opening up. Social opening up also brought about freedom of literary creation. Following the emerging trend of freedom, Bei Dao and Mang Ke founded and published the private magazine *Today* in 1978. Many young poets began to publish poems with special images, abundant meanings and obscure connotations in *Today*, breaking with the unified artistic criteria since the 1950s and extensively absorbing nutrition from Western modern poetry. These poems also manifest anti-authority and political consciousness and embody serious reflection on and criticism of the social disaster, consciously shouldering the historical task of rebuilding poets' egos, returning to human nature in poetry and reshaping artistic aesthetics. The development of these poems aroused extensive attention from researchers at that time. In 1980, these poems were called "obscure poetry" for the first time.

"Obscure poetry" originated earlier from "underground poetry" during the "Cultural Revolution." Famous "underground poets" such as Shi Zhi laid a spiritual foundation for later creation of "obscure poetry." Shi Zhi, with the original name of Guo Lusheng, adopted the form of free-style new poetry and summarized the mental pain felt by idealistic young people in their fall into the abyss. He had a clear understanding of the Cultural Revolution, and expressed thorough disappointment about and sharp criticism of the Cultural Revolution. This was quite commendable and precious at that time. Hand-written copies of Si Zhi's poems such as *Fish Trilogy*, *This is Beijing at 4:08* and *Believe in the Future* were circulated by numerous young people and struck a responsive chord with people in the period of explosion of Cultural Revolution slogans.

This is Beijing at 4:08 is a poem embodying the spirit of the times. In the poem, the author fully expressed his helplessness and sadness in the face of departure and his bewilderment and unexplainable pain in the face of future uncertainties.

Beijing station's towering edifice
Convulses without warning
Shaken, I look out the windows
Not knowing what's going on
My heart shudders in pain; it must be
My mother's sewing needle runs me through
At this moment my heart transforms into a kite
Tethered to her hands
Beijing still underfoot
Slowly begins to drift away
Once more I wave to Beijing
And I want to grab her by the collar
And shout to her
Remember me, Mother Beijing!

Shi Zhi compared Beijing to his mother. Leaving Beijing is like a helpless and fearful child's departure from his mother, and the train is like a stranger's hand taking away the child from his mother by force. The poem describes the complex feeling that the generation of educated youth had

Shu Ting

Photo of poets including Bei Dao, Shu Ting and Gu Cheng

before going to the mountains and the countryside. It was not only individuals' pain in life, but also the great pain of the times. However, when ideals were disillusioned and the future was extremely misty, the poet proved the value of this generation's existence with the poem. Such spirit of still cherishing ideals resolutely in despair also became the most precious spiritual treasure for "obscure poetry" that emerged later.

After the Cultural Revolution ended, "underground poetry" began to float to the historical surface, and the "obscure poetry" movement also began. Representative poets included Bei Dao, Gu Cheng, Mang Ke, Duo Duo, Shu Ting, Jiang He, Yang Lian, Hai Zi, etc. Mang Ke was one of the founders of the magazine *Today*. He made prominent contributions both in the period of underground "obscure poetry" and after "obscure poetry" was officially recognized following the founding of *Today*. Mang Ke's poems are refreshing, natural, unrestrained and free like his behavior. When reading Mang Ke's poem, one seems to feel the fragrance of soil and feel very warm. The images full of vitality selected by him made people who suffered great oppression during the Cultural Revolution feel great strength. Mang Ke's representative poetry collections include *Selected Poems of Mang Ke*, *Sunflowers in the Sun*, etc.

Shu Ting, a representative of female poets in the "obscure poetry" movement, wrote poetry collections such as *The Two-Mast Ship* and *The Singing Flower*. She actively joined the *Today* poetry group, and became known for creating *To The Oak*:

If I love you
I won't wind upon you like a trumpet creeper
upvalue myself by your height
I will never follow a spoony bird
repeating the monotune song for the green shade
not only like a springhead
brings you clean coolness whole year long
I must be a ceiba by your side
as a tree standing together with you
we partake cold tide, thunder storm, firebolt

This is a bold declaration of love and the poet's pursuit of lofty character and women's value. Shu Ting's poems do not directly face the gloomy times but call for recovery of compassion and love from a woman's standpoint and protest against the times through eulogizing the dignity and rights of "people." Her romantic and elegant poems combining classical sentiments and modern thoughts and thoroughly expressing modern Chinese people's painful disillusionment brought about a refreshing trend in the heavily suppressed poetry circles then.

Though the "obscure poetry" movement did not last long, it occupies an important place in the history of Chinese modern poetry. "Obscure poems" inheriting the literary traditions of the "May 4th Movement" give emphasis to poetry's artistic value and attention to individuals' existence; they express discontent with politics, violently accuse the times of destruction of human nature, and pursue man's spiritual freedom and value of existence; they are deeply influenced by Western modernism and draw on the techniques of the modern school, bringing Chinese new poetry into line with the world.

Bei Dao: A Rational Poet

Poet Bei Dao at the survivors' poetry reading party in the spring of 1989

Bei Dao was a representative of "obscure poets," and the leading figure and spiritual leader of the "obscure poetry" movement. He opened the path of "obscure poetry" creation, and was one of the most prominent poets in the "obscure poetry" movement. Bei Dao began to create poems in the mid and late 1970s, and still creates poems today.

Bei Dao's poetry creations are divided into the early stage and the late stage with the late 1980s as the dividing point. In the early stage, he mainly created "obscure poems" represented by *The Answer*, *An End or a Beginning – for Yu Luoke*, *Résumé*, *Walking Toward Winter*, *Nightmare*, poetry collection *Notes from the City of the Sun,* etc. These poems express the poet's deep worries about the motherland and people's future and fate. Bei Dao sharply criticized the phenomenon of social injustice, and closely examined issues such as life, death, history and freedom. Sticking to ideals and yearning for common and peaceful life are also main themes of Bei Dao's "obscure poems."

The Answer is Bei Dao's representative work created in 1976 soon after the Cultural Revolution ended:

Debasement is the password of the base,
Nobility is the epitaph of the noble.
See how the gilded sky is covered
With the drifting twisted shadows of the dead.

The Ice Age is over now.
Why is there ice everywhere?
The Cape of Good Hope has been discovered.
Why do a thousand sails contest the Dead Sea?

I came into this world
Bringing only paper, rope, a shadow.
To proclaim before the judgement
The voice that has been judged:

Let me tell you, world.
I–do–not–believe!
If a thousand challengers lie beneath your feet,
Count me as number one thousand and one.

I don't believe the sky is blue;
I don't believe in thunder's echoes;
I don't believe that dreams are false;
I don't believe that death has no revenge.

If the sea is destined to breach the dikes
Let all the brackish water pour into my heart;
If the land is destined no rise
Let humanity choose a peak for existence again.

A new conjunction and glimmering stars

Adorn the unobstructed sky now;
They are the pictographs from five thousand years.
They are the watchful eyes of future generations.

In that period, "base people" were not hindered while "noble people" could only go to graves. The poet wanted to expose the mask of that period and let people see its despicable reality. He cried loud, "I–do–not–believe!" People sleeping in the dark were wakened, became sober again, and exposed the hypocrisy of the world. The poet did not believe anything in the world, and wanted to fight against the times resolutely as a challenger. *The Answer* with clear rebellious consciousness sharply criticizes the society. The poem uses a lot of artistic methods such as symbolization and metaphor, and its direct expression of emotions and epigrams full of philosophical meanings are extremely grim, full of grief and indignation, and extremely shocking.

Poetry collection *Notes from the City of the Sun* was created at the end of the 1970s, consisting of 14 short poems. Each poem only has one or two sentences or even one word. *Notes from the City of the Sun* attracts readers' attention with its novel form, and its lines full of philosophical meanings enhance its charm. The poet expressed his understanding and comprehension of life in this poetry collection. The last poem *Life* only has one word:

Net

No explanation is needed. The word "net" depicts the essence of life and expressed Bei Dao's deep understanding of life.

With the decline of the "obscure poetry" movement, Bei Dao created less and less works and even stopped creating works for a while. After he settled down abroad in 1989, he began to create poems again. His later poems inherit the linguistic style of his early poems but shift the focus from the society to individuals' life experiences and inner feelings, manifesting warmth in grimness. His long years of wandering overseas made "nostalgia" an important theme of Bei Dao's poems imperceptibly, and his poems were more and more permeated by the poet's love for his mother tongue. Important works written in this period include *A Local Accent*, *Going Home*, etc. *A Local*

Accent is as follows:

I speak Chinese to the mirror
a park has its own winter
I put on music
winter is free of flies
I make coffee unhurriedly
flies don't understand what's meant by a native land
I add a little sugar
a native land is a kind of local accent
I hear my fright
on the other end of a phone line

"A park" has its own "winter," but "I" cannot find my destination. "I" put on music and make coffee to alleviate my gloomy mood, but there is no effect. "I" am more miserable than "flies" that have no native land or pain of missing and live free and easy. The poet's self-mocking makes readers feel more grieved.

Bei Dao having ingenious imagination and profound thought made successful attempts to modernize poetry creation; he persistently loved Chinese, developed the potential of Chinese and made modern Chinese poems more expressive; he inherited the poetry traditions of the "May 4th Movement," reshaped humanistic spirit, and reached another peak of Chinese modern poetry's development. Bei Dao received the Swedish PEN Literary Award, the PEN Center USA West Award for Freelance Writing, the Guggenheim Fellowship, etc., was elected an honorary member of the American Academy of Arts and Letters, and won reputation around the world.

Gu Cheng: A Fairy Tale Poet

Gu Cheng

Gu Cheng born in an intellectual family was under good cultural influence in his childhood and had inherent refined emotions. He created the poem *Poplar* at the age of eight as a precocious poet. In his youth, sufferings in the Cultural Revolution cast inerasable shadows on his soul, and exerted huge influence on his later poetry creation. At the age of 12, Gu Cheng left the city and was sent to Shandong's countryside with his father. Blue skies, quiet clouds, flying girds, blooming flowers… Gu Cheng experienced joy and happiness in nature. In 1977, Gu Cheng began to write a lot of poems and became one of the representative poets in the "obscure poetry" movement. He went abroad to give lectures in 1987, arrived in New Zealand then, and lived in seclusion on Waiheke Island away from people later to build life like a fairy tale in his imagination. In 1993, Gu Cheng committed suicide after killing his wife, ending his life in a violent way. The real reason why he killed himself is still a mystery. "You believed in the fairy tale written by you, and you became an orchid in the fairy tale." Shu Ting dedicated this poem titled *Fairy Tale Poet* to Gu Cheng, hence Gu Cheng's nickname "Fairy Tale Poet."

Gu Cheng's poems can be classified into two categories

according to themes and contents. Poems of the first category give attention to the world, nature and self from children's perspective, and in these poems the world is as pure and peaceful as in fairy tales, represented by *Night of the Countryside, Recollection, Nameless Flowers, Life Fantasia, I am a Willful Child*, etc. In works of the second category, Gu Cheng paid attention to the society and thought about life. Some poems have certain political meanings, express Gu Cheng's inquiries about history and social reality as well as his reflection on interpersonal relationships, and reveal philosophical meanings. The poem shows the poet's discontent with the current life, bewilderment, hesitation and longing for brightness. Representative works include *A Generation, Far and Near, Farewell to the Graveyard, On an Unfamiliar Street, End, Historical Civil War*, etc.

Even with these dark eyes, a gift of the dark night
I go to seek the shining light.

The poem *A Generation* only contains 18 Chinese characters, but every Chinese character goes straight to people's hearts. It greatly shocked the poetry circles then. The "dark night" refers to the suffocating society. In the "dark night," people felt downhearted, oppressed and painful. The "dark night" blinded people's eyes, so people could not see the future and life was void, solitary and lonely; however, the poet did not yield to all these brought to him by the "dark night" and wanted to seek the shining light with these "dark eyes." "Dark eyes" and "shining light" constitute a contradiction, but this irreconcilable contradiction and absurdity highlight the resolute resistance and persistent pursuit of ideals. The poem expresses the aspiration of "a generation" and portrays the spirit of this generation: though deeply wounded, bewildered and perplexed, they still resisted desperately against the predetermined fate like heroes. This poem shows a generation's incessantly rushing stream of life, and keeps inspiring later people to pursue human freedom indomitably.

Gu Cheng was also a poet retaining childlike innocence. He refused to grow up, and refused to enter adults' world. Bewildered by fairy tales, he always tried to build his own "fairy tale kingdom" in which there is no darkness or conflict and only simplicity and beauty. This characteristic is most obviously manifested in *I am a Willful Child*!

I am a willful child
I wish to erase all misfortunes
I wish to paint windows
All over the earth
So that all eyes that are used to the night
Would get used to the light
I am wishing
And wondering
But I don't know why
I haven't got the crayons
Nor a moment that is colored
I only have me
My fingers and my pains
So I have to tear up the paper piece by piece
My beloved white paper
Let them go after the butterflies
Let them disappear from the present

The poem epitomizes Gu Cheng's aesthetic ideals and persistent pursuit of ideals. He longed for a pure and harmonious world, "love without pain" and "eyes that never shed tears," but because ideals and reality could never be united, this "willful child" never got the crayons and could not draw this beautiful world. At last, he had to tear up "beloved white paper" piece by piece and let them "disappear from the present." However, "I" was still a "spoiled child" of the "imagined mother" and still persistently pursuing the beautiful world in imagination.

Hai Zi: The Catcher in the Rye

Hai Zi

Hai Zi was one of the most important poets in the late stage of the "obscure poetry" movement. He passed the entrance examination of the Law Department of Peking University in 1979 at the age of 15, and began to create poems in his university years. On March 26, 1989, Hai Zi laidhimself on railway tracks near Shanhaiguan to commit suicide at the young age of 25.

Hai Zi's poems with emphasis on poetic rhetoric are characterized by beautiful and elegant language, recommending the state of transcending secular customs. Relying on his glorious talent, his ingenious imagination and creativity and his extraordinary diligence and will, he completed poems, novels, dramas and dissertations with a total length of nearly 2 million Chinese characters in his short life. Hai Zi was deeply influenced by German poet Hölderlin and philosopher Heidegger, and unable to restrain his feeling for unexplainable mysterious things. Therefore, his poems often pursue the spiritual experience of integration between God's words and man's words. Under the poet's pen, the night often mysteriously integrates with harvests, land and skies.

In his poems, Hai Zi persistently stuck to ideals,

exploration of the spiritual world and the essence of art and the pursuit of life values. The three main themes of Hai Zi's more than 300 short lyric poems and long poem *The Sun – Seven Books* are: painful pursuit of love, obsession with and praise of land, and reflection on life and death.

Love is an important theme of Hai Zi's poems. Hai Zi fell in love four times in his lifetime but failed every time. In love, Hai Zi was a failure, so he sank into deep pain. Hai Zi's love poems are simple and sweet. Some are touching and romantic, but more of them express his pain, struggle, pursuit of perfect love and the sadness and despair brought by his failure to get love. For example, *Four Sisters* is a poem full of desperate cries, showing the poet's loneliness and pain in front of love. The "four sisters" are embodiments of the four women Hai Zi loved, and that "desperate" wheat head is perhaps a symbol of life, expressing his sadness brought by love. Hai Zi's love poems do not pursue aesthetically pleasing language or purposely pursue passionate release of emotions but combine truth, goodness and beauty and manifest the glory of human nature.

Obsession with and praise of land is another theme of Hai Zi's poems. For example, "All brothers in the world will embrace in wheat fields in the east, south, north and west, and four good brothers in wheat fields recalling the past and reciting their poems will embrace in wheat fields" (*Wheat Field in May*); "Existence does not need to be perceived for land shows it itself, and happiness and pain are also used to rebuild the homeland's roofs; contemplation and wisdom are abandoned: if you cannot bring wheat ears, please face land honestly, remain silent and maintain your dark nature" (*Rebuilding the Homeland*). Hai Zi was a farmer's son. "Land" fostered his body and sheltered his soul. Hai Zi was an urban vagrant and could hardly integrate into urban life. The nature and countryside not opened up by the modern civilization became Hai Zi's eternal spiritual homeland. He was obsessed with land and villages, eulogized harmonious and quiet rural life, showed deep love for the agricultural society, and looked for his spiritual destiny in it.

Besides, Hai Zi also reflected on life and death in poems – for example, long poems *River, September, Poem of Death* and *Song of the Suicide*. He was concerned about human life and its relationship with history. Among Hai Zi's such poems and even all his poems, the most widespread one is the short lyric poem *Facing the Sea, with Spring Blossoms* created in 1989:

From tomorrow on,
I will be a happy man;

Grooming, chopping,
and traveling all over the world.
From tomorrow on,
I will care foodstuff and vegetable,
Living in a house towards the sea,
with spring blossoms.
From tomorrow on,
write to each of my dear ones,
Telling them of my happiness,
What the lightening of happiness has told me,
I will spread it to each of them.
Give a warm name for every river and every mountain,
Strangers, I will also wish you happy.
May you have a brilliant future!
May you lovers eventually become spouse!
May you enjoy happiness in this earthly world!
I only wish to face the sea, with spring flowers blossoming.

The "sea" is an important image in this poem. The "sea" was the poet's spiritual home and the place where he placed his ideals. "Facing the sea" could let the poet feel peace, while "spring blossoms" could bring warmth and hope. Hai Zi lived alone in his lifetime, solitary and lonely. He was eager to communicate with people and be an ordinary person, but he could hardly bear the noisy and trivial family life and ultimately still returned to the secular living state and mental state. The poet expressed good wishes for everything in the world but still chose to "face the sea with spring blossoms." This poem with plain and refreshing language depicts the real and vivid secular life full of vitality in the poet's imagination, expresses the poet's longing and yearning for secular common life, embodies the poet's good wishes for the world, and reflects the poet's sincere and kind soul.

Hai Zi's creations not only belong to a period, but also are eternal poems of mankind. Therefore, Hai Zi was an important and indispensable poet in the history of Chinese modern poetry.

New Period – Diversified Novels

In the new period, an abundance of novels were created. Liu Xinwu's short novel *The Headmaster* pioneered "trauma literature;" Gao Xiaosheng's *Li Shunda Builds a House*, Ru Zhijuan's *A Wrongly Edited Story*, Zhang Jie's *Heavy Wings*, Jia Pingwa's *A Family in Jiwowa*, Tie Ning's *Ah, Xiangxue*, Chen Rong's *Upon Reaching Middle Age*, Gao Xiaosheng's *Chen Huansheng Going to Town*, Li Cunbao's *Wreaths at the Foot of the Mountain*, Acheng's *Chess Master*, Mo Yan's *Red Sorghum*, Liu Suola's *You Have No Other Choice*, Wang Meng's *The Man with Movable Parts*, Ma Yuan's *Fabrication*, etc. display and reflect various aspects of the times and society from diversified perspectives in an all-round manner, showing the unprecedented prosperous scene of novel creation. At the turn of the century, a new journey of novel creation began, and Yu Hua's *To Live*, Wang Xiaobo's T*he Golden Age*, Chen Zhongshi's *White Deer Plain*, Wang Anyi's *The Eternal Regret*, Su Tong's *Rice*, Zhang Jie's *Without Words*, Bi Feiyu's *The Plain*, Mo Yan's *Frog*, etc. all exerted important influence. It should be noted that some weighty works also emerged among Internet novels with extensive influence – for example, Ning Ken's *The Covered City* became one of the long novels that won the 2002 "Lao She Literary Award."

Jia Pingwa and Root-seeking Novels

The 800-li Qinchuan is plain and mysterious with a long history and profound cultural connotations. The land full of charm also nourished a group of writers with the same charm including Jia Pingwa. Jia Pingwa grew up in a poor peasant family in Shaanxi, and began his creation career in 1972. Jia Pingwa's creations are full of regional color. His hometown Shangzhou is not only the background of his writing, but also provides abundant materials for him. His talent and rebellious spirit also make his works' styles diversified and the contents colorful.

Jia Pingwa is a versatile and productive writer. After he entered the literary circles, his short novel *Full Moon* aroused attention. After 1983, he successively released novels related to changes in the life of farmers in Shangzhou, Shaanxi such as *The Story of Xiaoyue*, *A Family in Jiwowa*, *The Last and First Months of a Year*, *Distant Mountains and Wild Passions*, *Sky Dog*, *Black Clan*, *The Ancient Fortress*, *Shangzhou* and *Turbulence*, which are called novels of the "Shangzhou series" and are Jia Pingwa's representative works. He wanted to "experience, study, analyze and dissect Chinese rural areas' historical development, social transformation and life change in Shangzhou." Later he created novels such as *Deserted City* and *Shaanxi Opera*, manifested his unique style more obviously, and exerted great influence among readers.

Turbulence truly manifests the life scene of

Jia Pingwa's novels *Shaanxi Opera*, *Turbulence* and *Deserted City*

a relatively closed town's society in the early period of reform and opening up with the protagonist Jin Gou's tough experiences as the main clue. The novel's title "turbulence" is a symbolic summary of the feeling of the times and the mentality of the nation with abundant ideological and cultural connotations. This novel won the U.S. Mobil Pegasus Prize for Literature in 1987.

Shaanxi Opera won the 7th Mao Dun Literature Prize in 2008. The story of the novel takes place in Qingfeng Street. The generous and upright old director Xia Tianyi has led ordinary people of Qingfeng Street through decades of wind and rain, and has loved land all his life. When seeing Xia Junting's irrational commercial development of land harm villagers' life, he feels extremely painful. Xia Tianyi dies in a mud slide on the land loved by him. This also suggests how the traditional mode of agricultural production will end at last. The new branch secretary Xia Junting having received modern education can eliminate the restrictions of traditional views and has modern production consciousness and commercial consciousness. He establishes a free market of agricultural products in Qingfeng Street but ultimately fails because of lack of information and poor sales; the old headmaster of noble character and high prestige Xia Tianzhi loves Shaanxi opera and regards it as his life but can only helplessly see this ancient form of traditional Chinese opera decline and see rural simplicity gradually disappear. Xia Tianzhi is a representative of the traditional culture. Through depicting his fate, the author expressed his worries about the fate of the traditional culture. In the novel, the development of love between the "madman" Yinsheng and Bai Xue is a clue linking the stories happening in Qingfeng Street. In people's eyes, the "madman" Yinsheng is the story narrator and often flashes extraordinary wisdom while speaking wildly, adding mysterious color to the novel.

Jia Pingwa's novels focus on Chinese countryside in the reform and opening up period with Shangzhou as the main background of creation. They have strong regional color, are full of folk customs, manifest the anxiety and pain shown by Chinese people in social transformation, and have far-reaching significance. Because of the profound cultural connotations, his novels also have important folk value. With these characteristics, he formed a style of his own in the modern literary circles in the new period and occupied an important place in the history of Chinese modern literature.

In the mid-1980s, the conspicuous phenomenon of seeking cultural roots emerged in China's literary circles. The emergence of root-seeking consciousness on the one hand was the result of literature's development in the new period, and on the other hand was brought about by foreign literature's stimulation, especially the influence of Latin American hallucinatory realism. With the continuous deepening of ideological emancipation, literature gradually began to respect its aesthetic nature, and a number of works with different aesthetic tastes and artistic styles emerged in the literary circles – for example, Wang Zengqi's *Becoming a Monk*, Liu Shaotang's *The Family under A Big Catkin Willow*, Deng Youmei's *The Snuff Bottle*, Jia Pingwa's *First Records of Shangzhou*, etc. brought about a refreshing trend in the literary circles then. In 1984, the long novel *One Hundred Years of Solitude* by Columbian writer and winner of the Nobel Prize in Literature Márquez was translated, introduced to China and evoked great repercussions. Such tapping of local culture and exploration of local culture achieved great success, complied with the strong wish of many Chinese writers of that period to examine the nation's reality with modern consciousness and tap and carry forward the nation's cultural traditions, and stimulated their awareness of participation in world literature hidden in their hearts. They attributed the success of Latin American literature to the unique color of regional culture, and began to turn their eyes to Chinese rural, folk and primitive culture not affected by modern civilization and explore the origin and essence of national culture in the regional life they were familiar with in an attempt to seek emancipation of literary views in a more fundamental sense and reshape national spirit. Han Shaogong's "random talk" series of novels, Li Yuhang's "Gechuan River" series of novels, Jia Pingwa's "Shangzhou" series of novels, Zheng Wanlong's "strange tales from strange lands" series of novels, Acheng's novel series entitled *Romances of the Landscape*, Zheng Yi's *Remote Village and Old Well*, Mo Yan's *Red Sorghum*, Zheng Chengzhi's *River in the North*, etc. all reflect this view on novels. Most of these works manifest folk customs and people's livelihood, examine them historically as cultural phenomena, reflect the nation's cultural psychology and have strong regional color.

Yu Hua and Vanguard Novels

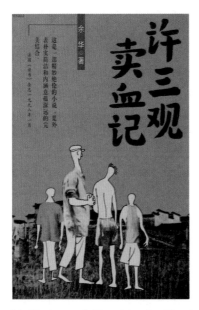

Yu Hua's novel *Chronicle of a Blood Merchant*

Yu Hua, a native of Hangzhou, Zhejiang, grew up mainly in Haiyan County. Yu Hua says in his autobiography, "I lived in Haiyan for nearly 30 years. I am familiar with everything there… All my past inspiration is from there, and my future inspiration will also come from there." In 1984, Yu Hua published his first novel *Stars* and began to reveal his uniquely individualized literary talent. Later he published works such as *A Kind of Reality*, *A World of Affairs like Smoke* and *A Story Dedicated to the Girl Willow* successively, carried out bold practice in the field of vanguard novels, and formed a style of his own. Under Yu Hua's pen, the cruel interpersonal state is outlined easily in an unrestrained atmosphere. After the 1990s, the style of Yu Hua's creation changed greatly. He began to pay attention to ordinary people's daily life and feelings, and completed long novels such as *To Live*, *Chronicle of a Blood Merchant* and *Brothers*. Though still having the characteristic of "violent" narration, they are more focused on manifesting tender interpersonal feelings and eulogizing man's kind and noble character.

To Live is one of Yu Hua's important representative works about the hard life of Fugui's family. Fugui is a landlord's son. After he gambles away the entire family fortune in his

youth, his father dies with indignation. Later he is forced to join the Kuomintang army and fight on the battleground, and is captured by the Liberation Army. By the time he finally returns home, he finds that his mother has died and that his daughter Fengxia has become deaf and mute. Years later, his son Yongqing dies while donating blood to the county head's wife due to excessive withdrawal of blood. Later he finds that the county head is Chunsheng, Fugui's comrade-in-arms in the Kuomintang army. Fugui and Chunsheng used to go through fire and water together. This is a heavy blow on Fugui. Several years, Fengxia dies from dystocia and leaves a poor newborn child and his wife Jiazhen also died of prolonged illness. However, this family's disasters are not over. His son-in-law dies tragically in an accident, and his daughter's son chokes to death while eating beans. Family members die one after another, and only Fugui lives and maintains optimistic and magnanimous forever. It seems that the author dared not "kill" Fugui and left some hope and imagination to readers. At the end of the novel, as Fu Gui and his old cow gradually go away, the author wrote, "the field gets quiet, the dusk passes in the blinking of an eye, and land is calling for the advent of night." Such time change of nature on the one hand suggests Fu Gui's life is about to end and at the same time heralds a new day's inevitable arrival. The author seems to want to tell people: no matter what happens and what hardship is encountered, tomorrow will be a new day, so we should live with strong will.

Chronicle of a Blood Merchant written in 1995 is another masterpiece written after Yu Hua's transition, epitomizing the author's sympathy with and compassion for hardships in ordinary people's life, his sigh over the fleetness of fate and his in-depth examination of and care for Chinese history and society. The protagonist Xu Sanguan overcomes many disasters in life through "selling blood" in exchange for continuation of his family's life, showing the sadness and helplessness of modern people facing difficult situations. Meanwhile, the novel also tells people: only by treating people around them with a warm attitude and helping others generously can they live with dignity without getting lost in cold life.

Yu Hua is one of the Chinese writers most reputed in the world. The U.S. *Time* magazine evaluated his *To Live* and *Chronicle of a Blood Merchant*: they "encompass the collective tragedy of China's 20th century and will help one of China's top writers gain the international recognition he deserves." Yu Hua's works have been translated into English, French, German, Italian, Spanish, Japanese and Korean and published abroad. He won the Italian Grinzane Cavour Prize, the

Still of film *To Live* adapted from Yu Hua's novel with the same title

Australian "Suspended Sentence Award" and the French Order of Arts and Letters, and became a very active representative writer of new novels in China's modern literary circles. His *To Live* was also adapted into a film with the same title and evoked extensive responses

The first attempts to write Chinese modern vanguard novels were made by Liu Suola, Xu Xing and Ma Yuan in the mid-1980s and Hong Feng, Yu Hua, Su Tong, Ge Fei, Ye Zhaoyan, etc. in the late 1980s. The biggest difference between vanguard novels and previous ones is that vanguard novels shift from describing the experiential world of man's external behavior to careful exploring man's subjective world. They include man's subjective stream of consciousness and perverted psychologies and feelings into the scope of literary manifestation, and deepen the understanding of man and the expression of the rich and complex inner world.

You Have No Other Choice, Liu Suola's first work and representative work, is a pioneering work in the development of vanguard novels. The novel depicts the life of a group of young students at an academy of music like a farce, and reveals to us their deep loneliness, emptiness of doing nothing, bewildered and agitated mentality, unstoppable creative passion and persistent pursuit. The novel manifests a strong sense of modernity, and answers fundamental questions that modern philosophy is concerned about such as "What am I?", "What is man?" and "What are

nature and environment?"

Ma Yuan is another representative writer of vanguard novels. Novel collections *Temptation of Gangdese* and *Fabrication* and long novel *Flat Up and Down* are his representative works. Ma Yuan's novels boldly attempt to use the narrative mode of Western structuralism and at the same time focus on his own existential experience as well as narration's non-causality, non-continuity, randomness and unpredictability. He purposely created the artistic effect of fabrication and distortion to eliminate the meanings of contents themselves and leave space for equivocal association and interpretation to readers.

Besides, vanguard writers were also accustomed to tapping the "abnormal" side of love in an attempt to resist inhibition of people's hearts by the traditional concept of love. Ye Zhaoyan's *The Shop at the Crossroad*, Ge Fei's *First Lover*, etc. challenge the model of traditional love novels, cause complete deconstruction of love, and expose the other side of love, marriage and families that people do not want to see like a beautiful, magnificent and exquisite pagoda. However, it collapses after a light blow!

Vanguard novelists also had special thoughts about death, and elaborated that death was another kind of reality in the world and another kind of secret anguish in the depths of people's souls. Yu Hua clearly tells us in *To Live* and *Chronicle of a Blood Merchant* that man obtains dignity through struggling with death. Vanguard novels survey the state of ordinary people's existence and man's spiritual essence in great depth with death as the breakthrough point.

Su Tong and New Historical Novels

Su Tong began to create and publish literary works in 1983 at the age of 20. His first medium-length novel *Escape of 1943* written between the autumn and winter of 1986 has unique historical meanings. Su Tong's main representative works include *Opium Family*, *Rouge*, *Wives and Concubines*, *Rice*, *Divorce Guide*, *Binu*, etc.

Su Tong used flowery and romantic language to build a beautiful and elegant "southern world" in his novels. The author directly depicted people leading secular lives in this "southern world," and wrote about their understanding of life, their questions about existence and their complex and subtle subconscious world. "Escaping" is an image frequently appearing in Su Tong's novels, e.g. escaping from the hometown and escaping from the countryside to a city. He created a series of characters "on the run" and a group of vagrants having lost their living space or spiritual home. They resist the mediocre and boring life and the predetermined fate and look for a new way out but do not know the direction. Su Tong sang many sad plaintive songs for them. Another characteristic of Su Tong's novels is that they shape many full-fledged women's images. These women are no longer angels always pure and nice or ideological pioneers manifesting

Cover of Su Tong's novel *Binu*

women's emancipation and fighting against men's oppression but women sunk into trivial life. They are eager to live and experience inner struggles, but they finally lose themselves, submit to the current status of their existence and stage tragedies of fate time and again.

More uniquely and importantly, Su Tong's creations link and traverse history and reality, and establish his own understanding of the meaning of life, social evolution and historical development.

Wives and Concubines is one of Su Tong's representative works. The story of the novel happened in the 1920s. The protagonist Songlian is an educated "new woman." Her family declines when she is 19 years old. To ensure sufficient food and clothing, she abandons the dignity and pursuit of "new women," voluntarily accepts old-style marriage, and becomes the fourth wife in the Chen family, a big feudal family with traditions inherited generation after generation. Though it is very rich, its inhibition and devastation of human nature are beyond all proportions. The master of the Chen family sleeps with a different wife every night and hangs a big red lantern as a mark. The frequency of hanging the big red lantern represents how favored that wife is, and thus she gets power or loses power. This phenomenon in the Chen family typically represents extension of traditional forces in Chinese feudal society to modern society. This living environment causes Songlian's self-respect to gradually disintegrate. She gradually participates in the cruel open strife and veiled struggle among the wives for winning favor. After watching many women being thrown into the deep well, Songlian feels afraid and desperate and becomes a lunatic at last. The novel explores the state of women's existence, describes women's psychological struggle in detail and in depth, and depicts the tragedy of many Chinese women's fate and life. In 1991, film director Zhang Yimou adapted it into the film *Raise the Red Lantern*, highlighted the specific historical scene, and achieved a strong artistic effect.

In *Binu*, Su Tong brings us back to remote antiquity. Lady Meng Jiang is an amazing woman who is loyal to love and travels one thousand li on foot to bring winter clothes to her husband in an ancient Chinese legend. Her story is known by almost all Chinese people. In this "myth-retelling" novel, Su Tong changed the name of the protagonist from Lady Meng Jiang to Binu. In the novel, Binu's tenacity and loyalty defeat secular conspiracies and ugly human nature. This woman at the bottom of the society oppressed by power and influence creates a myth-like legend with her love and kindness in troubled times. Su Tong thinks he never wanted to subvert the story of Lady Meng Jiang. "I will not adopt the method of deconstruction to change people's impression

Still of film *Raise the Red Lantern* adapted from Su Tong's novel *Wives and Concubines*

of Lady Mengjiang's beautiful legend. My novel undoubtedly tends to express feelings with 'tears.' The essence of Lady Meng Jiang's weeping at the Great Wall is 'weeping.' I focus on studying tears. This novel can be called a history of tears, describing various postures, types and origins of weeping." This shows Su Tong is different from many "myth-retelling" Western writers in that he does not deconstruct myths through later modern methods but highlights the most moving characters and scenes in myths through his understanding of history and thus reveals the value and significance of history and myths to the present age.

It is just in this sense that Su Tong's creation is associated with neo-historicism, so he is also regarded a representative writer of neo-historical novels. Neo-historicism, born in the British and American cultural and literary circles in the 1970s and 1980s, advocates including historical survey into literary research, and points out that there is no "foreground-background" relationship between literature and history and that they interact on and influence each other. The most important significance of neo-historicism is that it eliminates the boundary between history and literature and no longer emphasizes the traditional concept and model of real history and fictional literature. It gives special attention to history also having people's subjective consciousness, which can help people expand and deepen their understanding and comprehension of history itself.

In the mid-1980s, neo-historical novels emerged in China. Mo Yan's *Red Sorghum* and the creations of Su Tong and others jointly manifest the basic characteristics of neo-historical novels: history is no longer simply recognized as certain figures or things that emerged in the past and can be interpreted from multiple perspectives such as the past, today, others and oneself; historical figures are not just specific individuals who emerged in history, and these individuals also embody certain common features of human nature and manifest the universal significance of culture; historical scenes are time-specific, particular and even non-recurrent, but literary imagination and association can make scenes go through history and link history and reality – for example, many historical scenes of the Great Wall can be reproduced and sublimated in people's imagination today. Su Tong writes in *Preface to Binu*:

> *In the mythical tale of Lady Meng Jiang, a woman's tears bring the Great Wall crashing down; it is an optimistic tale, not a sorrowful one. Rather than characterize it as a woman's tears bringing an end to the drawn-out search for her husband, we might say that those tears enable her to resolve one of life's great predicaments.*
> *I have seen the Great Wall, and I have visited the Lady Meng Jiang Temple. But I have never seen Lady Meng Jiang. Who has? She is set adrift in narrative history and takes on many forms. I have attempted to give her a rope, one that can stretch across two thousand years, allowing her to pull me along with her; like her, I want to go to the Great Wall.*

Su Tong's statement explains his understanding of neo-historicism very well, and his works also practice neo-historical views very well.

Mo Yan and Hallucinatory Realism

Mo Yan, a native of Gaomi, Shandong, was born in a peasant family. In his childhood, economic poverty and political oppression left painful memories to him, and these psychological traits directly influenced his later novel creation. In the early 1980s, Mo Yan's novels such as *The Transparent Carrot* aroused attention from the literary circles, and later he created many medium-length novels such as *Red Sorghum*, *Garden*, *Big Breasts & Wide Hips*, *The Garlic Ballads*, *Red Forest*, *Sandalwood Death* and *Frog*, manifesting intensive cultural reflection and magical artistic feelings. Mo Yan's novel creation is influenced by American writer William Faulkner and Columbian writer García Márquez. He tries to gain a new understanding of the Chinese nation's life consciousness and cultural psychology with a novel and fresh artistic feeling, and meanwhile he is rooted in the Chinese nation's soil, inheriting many expression methods of Chinese traditional literature in depth and revealing a unique mysterious sense in the course of exploring reality.

The Transparent Carrot is a representative of Mo Yan's early works. The novel depicts the Black Child, an image suffering great mental repression in hard times. The Black Child loses the warmth of his family in his childhood, hard life and inhuman labor cause him to lose normal intelligence and feelings, and he forms the habit of silent endurance in long suffering. He never speaks to others and seems to feel no pain even his hand is mutilated by a hot anvil. The girl Juzi is a symbol of good wishes and holiness in his eyes, but he only wants to enjoy such pleasure in the depths of his heart himself. When Juzi publicly expresses compassion for and sympathy with him, he bites Juzi's wrist surprisingly. His love and hate are both extremist and normal, which is the result of cruel distortion by life. However, at the same time, the Black Child also has an extraordinary perceptive ability. He can hear the sound of carrot leaves' growth. In his eyes, red carrots are crystal clear, emitting an exotic and beautiful light. The image of the Black Child not

only is a true picture of misery in reality, but also has surreal symbolic color like a fairy tale. In the novel, almost all visual, auditory and sensory forms are mobilized, and abundant contents of subjective psychological experience bring about the multilayered effect of metaphoric symbolism and realize great artistic tension of the objects of expression. The work negates and criticizes not only that period, but also the terrible alienation of human nature.

Red Sorghum prominently represents the transition of Mo Yan's novels from rational meditation to perceptual infatuation. The novel symbolizes the nation's courage, valor and strong vitality aroused in a special environment under heavy pressure from the wars, hardships and shackles of feudal ethical codes rather than depicting stories of resistance against Japan. The novel shows the nation's strong and invincible will to live with the life scene of bold and uninhibited people in Northeast Township of Gaomi, and typically represents the basic style of Mo Yan's novels. The novel with the nation's strong courage and will to live, die, love and hate like *red sorghum* as the keynote describes all Chinese peasants' real primitive cultural psychology through the special environment of war. The work focuses on revealing and proving certain organic spiritual association among a nation's past, present and future. No previous novel on the theme of resistance against Japan is as deep-going, peculiar and soul-stirring as Red Sorghum. Mo Yan's novels created in the new period represented by *Red Sorghum* have changed the path of Chinese traditional novels with their unique style and become milestones of novel creation in the new period.

Mo Yan's novels published abroad

Hallucinatory realism literature emerged and developed in Latin America in the 1940s and 1950s as a product of combination of Latin American realistic novels' traditions and national consciousness. The most representative work is *One Hundred Years of Solitude* by Columbian writer García Márquez, which tries to reflect the spirit of the times in a hallucinatory atmosphere, enhance national features, opposes blindly imitating Western modern literature, and advocate going deep into nature, history and tradition to discover the essence of life. Latin American hallucinatory realism also deeply influenced Chinese modern writers including Mo Yan. Inspired by *One Hundred Years of Solitude*, Mo Yan based himself on the daily life of his hometown's ordinary farmers, explored the roots of traditional culture in it, gained a new understanding of national culture and national life, integrated hallucinatory realism with folk stories, history and modern life, and created a magical world. The medium-length novel *The Transparent Carrot* mentioned above shows the salient characteristic of transition between unreal images and reality. The protagonist Black Child's behavioral mode is divorced from realistic possibility and has hallucinatory color. He can hear the sound of hairs falling to the ground and the vibration in the air caused by falling leaves; he grasps a red-hot anvil and does not drop it though yellow smoke rises from his burned hand. However, he is also an ordinary person in real life. After leaving that bridge opening, he feels cold and can no longer see that "transparent red carrot." The author wanted to demonstrate the mental distortion caused by the turbulent times to the child. The broken family and childhood without maternal love cause the Black Child's tenacity and stubbornness against pain in reality. The Black Child's world is very hallucinatory and mysterious but is not divorced from reality. This is just the unique artistic effect realized by Mo Yan relying on methods of hallucinatory realism. *Red Sorghum* draws on the hallucinatory techniques of Márquez and the stream of consciousness method of Falkner and adopts the structural model of fairy tales and fables, so it is full of symbols, metaphors, unreal images, etc. Forest-like red sorghum is itself a symbol of the Chinese nation's spiritual core, and the numerous characters and pictures are all full of profound implications. These enhance the profoundness of the whole work's connotations as well as its poetic appeal.

Mo Yan's novels are deeply loved by Chinese and foreign readers. His *Big Breasts & Wide Hips* won the first "Dajia Honghe Literature Prize" of China; *White Dog and the Swing* won the United Literature Prize of Taiwan; the film *Nuan* adapted from it won the Gold Kylin Prize at the 16th Tokyo International Film Festival. Besides, Mo Yan also won many honors such asthe French Order of Arts and Letters and the 13th Italian NONINO International Prize for Literature. *Red*

Still of film *Red Sorghum* adapted from Mo Yan's novel with the same title

Sorghum Clan, *Big Breasts & Wide Hips*, etc. have been translated into more than ten languages including English, French, German and Japanese and widely spread in the world. The publication of long novel *Frog* in 2009 represented another peak of Mo Yan's creation career, and it won the 8th Mao Dun Literature Prize in 2011. On October 11, 2012, Mo Yan won the Nobel Prize in Literature. According to the Swedish Nobel Prize in Literature Awarding Committee's evaluation, "with hallucinatory realism," Mo Yan "merges folk tales, history and the contemporary."

Concluding Remarks

Concluding Remarks: New Trends of Literature in the New Century

From the late 20th century to the early 21st century, China's economy grew rapidly, science and technology kept developing, consumer culture was increasingly influential, and electronic devices such as TV sets, computers and mobile phones were widely popularized and became indispensable communication and entertainment tools in people's life. The emergence of new media such as the Internet broadened people's vision and diversified people's life. Chinese society entered a period of highly enriched material and cultural life. Meanwhile, emerging literary power also began to burgeon and grow. The most prominent phenomena were "youth writing" and "Internet literature."

In the new century, young people born in the 1980s gradually became mature, played important roles in social life, and showed their individuality, talent and ability. These young people are called "post-80s." As a group, "post-80s" and "post-90s" have some common characteristics: most of them have no sibling, enjoy comfortable living conditions, and have simple life experiences; are well educated and have a deep understanding of campus life; are well informed, have broad vision and can effectively obtain information and materials on the Internet. "Post-80s" and "post-90s" emerged in the literary circles, their literary works gradually entered people's sight and won young readers' favor, and "youth writing" suddenly became a vogue and reality.

In the tide of "youth writing," Han Han, Guo Jingming, Zhang Yueran, Jiang Fangzhou, Li Shasha, Chun Shu, Xu Peng, Liu Weidong, etc. are outstanding leading figures. Their works mostly manifest the details of campus life and adolescents' growing pains, show young and romantic colors, and at the same time reveal some decadent feelings. They make great efforts to display their personalities in their works, and manifest their attempt to subvert traditional values and break with conventional thoughts and tendencies. However, "post-80s" writers' creation styles are not the same, and different writers have different characteristics. Among them, Li Shasha born in the country side is among the few "post-80s" writers from the countryside. His novels are full of young vitality with precise and flowery language, and his prose works are refreshing and plain, making readers feel peace and distance from the maddening crowd. His representative works include long novel *Red X*. Zhang Yueran is loved by readers for exquisite description of details, use of novel and diversified images and the sincere writing attitude. Her works record the psychological path of young people's growth, and sincerely manifest adolescents' desire and pursuit. Her representative works include *Sunflower Missing in 1890* and *Oath Bird*. Jiang Fangzhou graduated from Tsinghua University. As a precocious and intelligent writer, she completed prose collection *Unlatched the Window onto the Paradise* at the age of 9, completed long novel *We are Growing* at the age of 11, and later published works such as *The Rainbow Rider*, *Number One Schoolgirl* and *Features of Rumors* successively. She breaks with the traditional writing mode, and his easy and casual words seem disorderly but are free, intelligent and novel to readers.

Among "post-80s" writers, Han Han and Guo Jingming have the most extensive influence in the society and are also fashion figures active in various media. Han Han is a race car driver, writer and magazine editor. He began to write in junior high school, won first prize in the first "New Concept Writing Competition" with his essay *Seeing Ourselves in a Cup* in 1999, and aroused attention from the literary circles. In the same year, Han Han in Senior Grade 1 chose to leave school and began his career of free writing. He successively published novels such as *Triple Door, Riot in Chang'an City, A Fortress, Glory Days* and *1988: I Want to Talk with the World* and novel collections such as *One Degree Below Freezing, Press Release 2003* and *And I Drift*. His representative work *Triple Door* manifests parent-child relations, teacher-student relations and classmate relations in young people's life from a high school student's perspective, and struck a responsive chord with teenager readers. In addition, the novel obviously uses oral language and is humorous. After being published, it became a bestseller, was later adapted into a TV series, and evoked great repercussions. Guo Jingming is not only a writer, but also a businessman and editor. His representative works include novels *The City of Fantasies, Left Hand Shadow, Right Hand Years and Never Flowers in Never Dream*, prose collection *The Edge of Love and Pain*, musical novels *Hide-and-seek* and *Sword Heroes' Fate*, and the *Island* magazine series edited by him.

Different from Han Han's sharp and jocose style, Guo Jingming's works show self-pitying and even narcissistic sentiments. His language is beautiful, classical, pure, elegant, and full of lonely and sad emotions. This keynote just conforms to adolescents' psychological state and touches young readers' hearts.

Today, "post-80s writing" has become a literary phenomenon in China's modern literary circles that cannot be ignored. As writers such as Chun Shu, Han Han and Li Shasha appeared on the front cover of the U.S. *Time* magazine, the world also began to pay attention to the growth of China's new generation of writers.

In the new century, "Internet literature" as a new literary form also rose quietly and kept developing. The popularization of the "Internet" brought new media carriers and dissemination modes for literature. Many Internet writers, especially "post-80s" and "post-90s" writers, began to publish their original works in the virtual space of the Internet, and carried out literary interaction. Blogs, forums, bulletin boards and some special websites have become platforms for communication of the latest Internet works.

As an emerging literary form, Internet literature has its salient features different from traditional literature. First, because of the open and virtual nature of the Internet, the existence of Internet literature is destined to be relatively free, so the success rate of works released by ordinary writers is much higher. After an original literary work is released, readers can give responses immediately and even directly participate in creation, so original literary works can be revised more freely. However, as a result of the existence of freedom, many Internet literary works do not have high quality and are even vulgar. This is also an important problem of Internet literature. Second, Internet literature manifests the mental attitude of resisting nobility in a certain sense. In comparison with traditional literature pursuing spiritual value of works and elegant linguistic styles, Internet literature is more prone to getting closer to ordinary people's daily life. To subvert traditional values, a lot of Internet literary works deconstructing classics have emerged. In terms of contents, Internet literature gives top priority to entertainment and amusement, and ridicule, derision and irony have also become their important linguistic characteristics. Third, the themes of Internet literature are diversified and the forms are flexible and numerous. Among them, "Internet novels" are most numerous and influential. According to themes, they can be classified into time-travel novels, love novels, officialdom novels, fantasy novels, swordsman novels, historical novels, tomb-raid novels, etc.

In the course of Internet literature's development, "Internet writers" have played a critical role. From the 1990s to now, Internet writers became popular one batch after another, received social attention and won readers' recognition, but their works have short lifespans. Though there are a lot works, they usually do not last long.

As a new literary phenomenon, Internet literature has injected fresh blood into China's literary circles. At present, the development of Internet literature is not mature. Though there are excellent works, a lot of shoddy works also exist. How to correctly guide the development of Internet literature is an important issue facing the present era and society.

Appendix:

Chronological Table of the Chinese Dynasties

Old Stone Age	Approx. 1,700,000-10,000 years ago
New Stone Age	Approx. 10,000-4,000 years ago
Xia Dynasty	2070-1600 BC
Shang Dynasty	1600-1046 BC
Western Zhou Dynasty	1046-771 BC
Spring and Autumn Period	770-476 BC
Warring States Period	475-221 BC
Qin Dynasty	221-206 BC
Western Han Dynasty	206 BC-AD 25
Eastern Han Dynasty	AD 25-220
Three Kingdoms	AD 220-280
Western Jin Dynasty	AD 265-317
Eastern Jin Dynasty	AD 317-420
Northern and Southern Dynasties	AD 420-589
Sui Dynasty	AD 581-618
Tang Dynasty	AD 618-907
Five Dynasties	AD 907-960
Northern Song Dynasty	AD 960-1127
Southern Song Dynasty	AD 1127-1279
Yuan Dynasty	AD 1206-1368
Ming Dynasty	AD 1368-1644
Qing Dynasty	AD 1616-1911
Republic of China	AD 1912-1949
People's Republic of China	Founded in 1949